Marriage Register
of
BERTIE COUNTY NORTH CAROLINA
- 1869-1872 -

(Volume #2)

Complied by:
Raymond Parker Fouts

Southern Historical Press, Inc.
Greenville, South Carolina

This volume was reproduced
from a personal copy located in
the Publishers private library

Please direct all correspondence and book orders to:
SOUTHERN HISTORICAL PRESS, Inc.
PO Box 1267
Greenville, SC   29602-1267

Copyright 1990 by: Raymond Parker Foutsr
Copyright Transferred 2023 to:
    Southern Historical Press, Inc.
ISBN #978-1-63914-248-4
Printed in the United States of America

PREFACE

This verbatim transcription is from microfilm reel C.010.63001, Bertie Marriage Register 1851-1917, obtained from the North Carolina State Archives, Raleigh, North Carolina.

The records herein were transcribed from the section of film described as "Bertie County Marriage Register 1851-1870", pages numbered 1-176, and "Bertie County Marriage Register 1870-1872", pages numbered 1-11. Beginning with 1851, certificates are numbered 1-871, ending on page 127. Page 128 is blank. The heading on page 129 is "Certificates of Marriges issued by E. S. SIMMONS Register of Deeds", and begins with certificate number 1, dated 3rd day of September 1868. Page 135 contains the first certificate for 1869. Certificates were recorded in the order in which they were returned and are not always in chronological order.

The Marriage Register for 1870-1872 is in a different format than that of the certificates. It is especially valuable to the researcher, as it gives the names of the parents of both brides and grooms. The columns extend the full width of two original pages. This arrangement has necessitated printing those pages on one, so as to be certain that they accurately represent the original.

Each original page has been assigned a number, in parentheses and bold print. The indices refer to these numbers. The page number of the original record is to the right of the assigned number and has been underlined. The certificate number precedes the surnames at the beginning of each entry. The certificate number and surnames are listed vertically in the original, but have been typed on one line in the interest of saving space on each page.

The word "Township" has been abbreviated "Twp." "B. Minister" has sometimes been abbreviated to "B.Min". === denotes letters or words crossed out, or erased, and illegible. Jose__ denotes missing letters. The letters "I" and "J" are indistinguishable. Some look-alikes are L=S; A=a; M=m. Underlined letters emphasize verbatim spelling. The abbreviations "Col" and "Cold" are underlined in the original. The abbreviation of Justice of the Peace is written (JP and has been represented here by (JP. A suggested source for determination of race of the celebrants is the Federal Census Schedule of 1870 and 1880 for Bertie County.

Marriages of Bertie County, North Carolina 1762-1868, compiled by Raymond Parker Fouts, Genealogical Publishing Co., Inc., copyright 1982, is available from that company, for readers interested in earlier marriages in this county.

TABLE OF CONTENTS

1869 1

1870 12

1871 22

1872 28

Groom Index 33

Bride Index 37

General Index 41

MARRIAGE REGISTER

OF

BERTIE COUNTY, NORTH CAROLINA

1869-June 1872

(1) 135
41 HARDY To HOLLY   I John W SESSOMS a Justice of the peace do hereby certify that I Solemnized the rightes (sic) of matrimony between Jas HARDY Col And Caroline HOLLEY on the 2 day of January 18689   John W SESSOMS (JP)

42 BASNETT To RAYNER   I George W COBB a Justice of the Peace do hereby certify that I solemnized the rites of matrimony between Jack BASNETT Col And Nancy RAYNER on the third day of January 1869   George W COBB (JP

43 WILLIAMS To CAPEHART   I Thadeous WILSON a minister of the Gospel do hereby Certify that Isolemnized th (sic) rites of matrimony between Sandy WILLIAMS Col and Celia CAPEHART Col on the 22 day of December 1868   Thaddus WILSON

44 COLLINS To JAMES   I Edward WOOTTEN a minister of the Gospel do hereby Certify that I solemnized the rites of matrimony between Prince A COLLINS Col and Mariah JAMES on the 28 day of December 1868   Edward WOOTTEN

45 SANDERS To HOLDER   I Jeremiah BUNCH a minister of the Gospel do hereby Certify that I solemnized the rites of matrimony between James E SANDERS And Fannie HOLDER on the 23 day of December 1868   Jeremiah BUNCH
Begin   [Written in margin.]

46 ROBBINS To SANDERLIN   I Thaddeus WILSON a minister of the Gospel do hereby Certify that Isolemnized the rites of matrimony between Samuel ROBBINS and Sue SANDERLIN Col on the 25. day of December 1868   Thaddeus WILSON

47 BUNCH To BACCUS   I Bryant LEE a minister of the Gospel do hereby Certify that I solemnized the rites of matrimony Between Jos W BUNCH Col And Lydia BACCUS on the 26 day of December 1868   Bryant LEE

(2) 136
48 CHERRY To CHERRY   I Bryant LEE do hereby certify that I Solemnized the rites of matrimony between Noah CHERRY Col and Rosa A CHERRY Col on the 26th day of December 1868   Bryant LEE

49 SHARP To RYAN   I Bryant LEE do hereby certify that I Solemnized the rites of matrimony between George SHARP Col and Gracy RYAN Col on the 24th day of December 1868   Bryant Lee

50 LOW To KING   I Thadeus WILSON a minister of the Gospel do hereby certify that I solemnized the rites of matrimony between John LOW Col and Judy KING of Col on the 25th day of December 1868   Thadeus WILSON

51 CAPEHART To CAPEHART   I Edward WOOTTEN a minister of the Gospel do hereby Certify that I Solemnized the rites of matrimony between Cademus CAPEHART And Mary M CAPEHART on the 28th day of December 1868   Edward WOOTTEN

52 GREGORY To WEBB   I Thadeus WILSON ======= a minister of the Gospel do hereby certify that I solemnized the rites

1869

52 (Cont.) of matrimoy Between Hubbard GREGORY Col and Pelelope WEBB Col on the 27 day of December 1868   Thadeus WILSON

52 (sic) ALAXANDER To OUTLAW   I Jeremiah BUNCH a minister of the Gospel do hereby Certify that I solemnized the rites of matrimony between Robert G ALAXANDER and Victoria R OUTLAW on the 29 day of December AD 1868   Jeremiah BUNCH

53   REED   To PUGH   I J SHEPPERD a Justice of the Peace do hereby Certify that I solemnized the rites of matrimony between Robert REED and Mary PUGH Col on the 30th of day (sic) of December 1868   John L SHEPPERD (JP

54   OUTLAW To ASKEW   I J W SESSOMS a Justice of the Peace do hereby certify that I solemnized the rites of matrimony Between William OUTLAW Col. and Renda ASKEW Col on the 2nd day of Jany 1869   J W SESSOMS (JP.

(3) 137
55   CLARK To SPRUILL   I William H BISHOP minister of the A M E Church do hereby Certify that I solemnized the rites of matrimony between George CLARK Col and Sallie SPRUILL 2 day of January 1869   signed   Wm H BISHOP

56   LINCH To BOND   I James H WARD a Justice of the peace do hereby certify that I solemnized the rites of matrimony between Henry LINCH and Albina BOND on the 28 day of January 1869   James H WARD JP

57   GILLAM To MITCHELL   I John MITCHELL a minister of the Gospel do hereby certify that I solemnized the rites of matrimony between Turner GILLAM Col and Rachel MITCHELL on the 6th day of January 1869   John MITCHELL

58   OUTLAW To CAPEHART   I Thadeous WILSON a minister of the Gospel do hereby certify that I solemnized the rites of matrimony between Alfred OUTLAW Col. and Julia A CAPEHART on the 7th day of January 1869   W Thad WILSON

59   JOHNSON To WALTON   I Edward WOOTTEN Priest hereby certify that I solemnized the rites of matrimony between James P JOHNSON and Agness WALTON on the Twenty Seventh day of January AD 1869   Edward WOOTTEN Presbyter of the P E Chu in [End of entry.]

60   CLARK To WYNN   I Richard E L COX do hereby certify that I Solemnized the rites of matrimony between Henry CLARK of Col and and (sic) Judy WYNN on the 22 day of February AD 1869   R. E. L. COX (JP

61   BURDEN To SLAUGHTER   I Bryant LEE a do hereby certify that I solemnized the rites of matrimony between George A BURDEN and Jane SLAUGHTER on the 9th day of January 1869   Bryant LEE Pastor

62   CHURCHWELL To WHITE   I Edward WOOTTEN a minister of the Gospel do hereby certify that I solemnized the rites of matrimony between William J CHURCHWELL and Martha E WHITE on the Fifth day of January 1869   Edward WOOTTEN

(4) 138
63   WEED To VERNOOY   I A M CRAIG a Minister of the Gospel do hereby Certify that I solemnized the rites of matrimony between Marcus A WEED and Miss Leah M VERNOOY on the 7th day of January 1869)   A. M. CRAIG

64   NICHOLLS To HARMAN   I John MITCHELL a minister of the Gospel do hereby Certify that I solemnized the rites of matrimony between Thos L NICHOLLS and Ann HARMAN on the 7th day of January 1869)   John MITCHELL

65   SPELLER To MC KLEESE   I James H WARD do a Justice of the Peace do hereby Certify that I solemnized the rites of matrimony between Sollomon SPELLER and Margaret MC KLEESE on the 20th of January 1869)   James H WARD JP

66   WHITE To NIXON   I Moses L MIZELL a minister of the Gospel do hereby certify that I solemnized the rites of matrimony between Joseph A WHITE And Sallie C NIXON on the Seventh day of January 1869   M L MIZELL

67   PENDER To BACCHUS   I John W SESSOMS a Justice of the Peace do hereby certify that I solemnized the rites of matrimony between Morriss PENDER and Patsey BACCHUS on the 9th day of Jany 1869   J W SESSOMS JP

1869

68 RAYNER To HOLLEY I George W COBB a Justice of the Peace do hereby Certify that I solemnized the rites of matrimony between Wright RAYNER And Malind HOLLEY on the Tenth day of Januay 1869 Geo W COBB JP

69 HOBBS To HARRELL I B B WILLIAMS a minister of the Gospel do hereby Certify that I solemnized the rites of matrimony between Charles C HOBBS and Ann M HARRELL on the 14th day of Januay 1869} B B WILLIAMS

70 MODLIN To HILL I John MITCHELL a minister of the Gospel do hereby certify that I Solemnized the rites of matrimony between Joseph MODLIN and Mary HILL on the 14th day of January 1869 John MITCHELL

(5) 139
71 WARD To ASKEW I Jeremiah BUNCH a minister of the Gospel do hereby Certify that I solemnized the rites of matrimony between George D WARD and Miss R E ASKEW on the 14th day of January 1869 Jeremiah BUNCH

72 PERRY To BACCUS I John W SESSOMS a Justice of the peace do hereby certify that Isolemnized the rites of matrimony between Elisha PERRY and Alice BACCHUS on the 23 day of Jany 1869} J W SESSOMS (JP

73 WILLIAMS To HINES I Thadeus WILSON a minister of the Gospel do hereby certify that I solemnized the rites of matrimony between Richard WILLIAMS col and Hannah HINES on the 13th day of Januay 1869} Thadeous WILSON

74 RUFFIN To RUFFIN I Robt W SMALLWOOD a Justice of the peace do hereby Certify that I solemnized the rites of matrimony between Abner RUFFIN And Abby RUFFIN on the 14th day of Febray 1869 Robt W SMALLWOOD (JP

75 MITCHELL To SESSOMS I B. B WILLIAMS a minister of the Gospel do hereby certify that I solemnized the rites of matrimony Between Thomas M MITCHELL and Mary P SESSOMS on the 17 day of Jany 1869 B. B. WILLIAMS

76 FRANKS To TREADWELL I Thadeus WILSON a minister of the Gospel do solemnized hereby Certify that I solemnized the rites of matrimony between Alfred FRANKS and Celia TREADWELL on the 17th day of January 1869} Thad WILSON

77 URQUHART To WATSON George BISHOP a Justice of the peace do hereby certify that I solemnized the rites of Matrimony between Alfred Slade URQUHART And Marietta WATSON on the 20th day of Januay 1869 George BISHOP (JP

78 WILKINS To TYLER I George BISHOP a Justice of the peac (sic) do hereby certify that I solemnized the rites of matrimony between Henry WILKINS and Rachel TYLER on the 23 day January 1869 George BISHOP (JP

(6) 140
79 TODD To DANIEL I Mosses L MIZELL a Minister of the Gospel do hereby Certify that I solemnized the rites of Matrimony between Korly TODD and Basha DANIEL on the Seventeenth day of Janary AD 1869 Moses L MIZELL

80 WILLIAMS To ROULHAC I James H WARD a Justice of the Peace do hereby Certify, that I Solemized the rites of Matrimony between Peter WILLIAMS Col and Eliza J ROULAC Col on the 25 day of Janary 1869 James H WARD (JP

81 WARSAW To SWAIN I James H WARD a Justice of the Peace do hereby Certify that I solemnized the rites of matrimony between Peter WARSAW And Louisa SWAIN Col on the 20th day of January 1869 Jas H WARD (JP

82 POWELL To RHODES I James H WARD a Justice of the Peace do hereby Certify that I Solemnized the rites of matrimony between Simon POWELL And Harriet RHODES on the 25 day of January 1869 J H WARD J.P.

83 RUFFIN To POWELL I Robt W SMALLWOOD JP do hereby Certify that I Solemnized the rites of matrimony Between Hilard RUFFIN And Mary Ann POWELL on the 17 day of January 1869 Robt W SMALLWOOD (JP

84 LIVERMAN To SADDLER I George BISHOP hereby Certify tha (sic) I Solemnized the rites of matrimony Between James H LIVERMAN And Sarah W SADDLER on the 20th day of January 1869 George BISHOP (JP

85 EVANS To WHITE I moses L MIZELL a minister of the Gospel do hereby certify that I solemnized the rites of matrimony between James H EVANS and Frances WHITE on the Twentieth day of January 1869 M L MIZELL

1869

86 URQUHART To VEALE   I George BISHOP a Justice of the Peace do hereby Certify that I solemnized the rites of matrimony between Wiley URQUHART And Rhody VEALE on the 23 day of January 18 1869 George BISHOP JP

(7) 141
867 BROWN To COX   I George BISHOP a Justice of the Peace do hereby certify that I Solemnized the rites of matrimony between Henry BROWN and Ellen COX on the 23rd day of January 1869 George BISHOP (JP

88 BROWN To RHODES   I Thadeus WILSON a minister of the Gospel do hereby certify that I solemnized the rites of matrimony between Washington BROWN And Harriet RHODES on the 23rd day of January 1869 Thadeous WILSON

89 HILL To WILLIAMS   I Benjamin CLARK do hereby Certify that I solemnized the rites of matrimony between ===== ========= Nead (or Neal) HILL col And Susan WILLIAMS on the 25 day of January 186 (sic) Signed Benjamin CLARK

90 PARKER To CHERRY   I Bryant LEE do hereby certify that I Solemnized the rites of matrimony between Fred PARKER and Feriby CHERRY on the 24 day of January 1869 Bryant LEE Pastor

91 CHERRY To ASKEW   I John MITCHELL (JP) hereby certify that I Solemnized the rites of matrinony between Ben CHERRY and Caroline ASKEW on the 28 day of January AD 1869 John MITCHELL (JP

92 GRAY To TREADWELL   I Thadeous WILSON a minister of the Gospel do hereby Certify that I Solemnized the rites of matrimony between Thomas GRAY col and Sarah TREADWELL on the ====== 15th day day (sic) of February 1869 Thadeous WILSON

93 HARRELL To RAYNER   I B. B WILLIAMS hereby certify that I solemnized the rites of Matrimony between George B HARRELL And Martha A RAYNER on the 27 day of January AD 1869) B. B. WILLIAMS MG

94 SMITH To MOORING   I John G MITCHELL hereby Certify that I solemnized the rites of matrimony between Turner SMITH col and Cornelia MOURNING col On the second day of December AD 1869 John G MITCHELL (JP

95 CAPHART To WESTON   I. J. W SMITH hereby certify that I solemnized the rites of matrimony between Wm A CAPEHART and Sallie W WESTON on the 16th December 1869 J W. SMITH JP

(8) 142
96 HOGGARD To RICE   I Bryant LEE D D do hereby Certify that I Solemniced the rites of matrimony between between (sic) Abel HOGGAR_ Col and Mary E RICE col on the 5th day of December AD 1869 (signed) Bryant LEE D D

97 BRIMAGE To MILLER   I Peter MOUNTAIN (JP) hereby certify that I solemni___ the rites of matrimony between BRIMAGE (sic) and Julia MILLER on the 12 day of December 186=9 (Signed) Peter MOUNTAIN JP

98 WILLIAMS To WILLIAMS   I Benjamin CLARK rev do hereby Certify that I Solemnized the rites of matrimony between Samuel WILLIAMS col And Rhany WILLIAMS on the 7th day of february 1869 (signed) Binjmin CLARK Rev

99 HARRELL To LIVERMAN   I John MITCHELL hereby certify that I solemnized the rites of Matrimony between Jos J HARRELL and Elizabeth LIVERMAN on the 11th day of Februay AD 1869 (sign) (sic) John MITCHELL

100 RUFFIN To RUFFIN   I Bryant LEE do hereby certify that I solemnized the rites of matrimony between Jessee RUFFIN col and Rhoda RUFFIN on the 13th day of February 1869 (Signed) Byant LEE

101 WINBON To THOMAS   I Robert W SMALLWOOD a Justice of the peace do hereby certify that I solemnized the rites of maty (sic) between John Henry WINBONE col and Amelia THOMAS col on the 14 day of february 1869 (signed) R W SMALLWOOD (JP

102 BURRESS To MILLER   I B B WILLIAMS a hereby (sic) certify that I solemnized the rites of matrimony between Joseph Joseph (sic) J BURRESS and Susan MILLER on the 14 day of February AD 1869 (signed) B. B. WILLIAMS MG

1869

103 HOLLEY To SMITH   I Edward WOOTTEN Presbyter hereby certify that I solemnized the rites of matrimony between Thos D HOLLEY And Eva M SMITH on the Twenty fifth day of february A.D. 1869 (signed) Edward WOOTTEN Presbyter

(9) 143
104 DAVIS To BUTLER   I Jeremiah BUNCH (a Minister) hereby Certify that I Solemnized the rites of matrimony between Allen DAVIS Jr. and Mrs. Eliza J BUTTER (or BUTLER) on the fifteenth day of February AD 1869   (Signed) Jeremiah BUNCH

105 OUTLAW To FREEMAN   I Benj B WILLIAMS hereby certify that I solemnized the rites of Matrimony Between Joseph W OUTLAW and Elizabeth C FREEMAN on the 21st day of February AD 1869 (Signed) B. B. WILLIAMS M. G.

106 TAYLOE To WESTON   I A minister of the Gospel do hereby certify that I solemnized the rites of matrimony between Henry TAYLOE And P. E WESTON on the Eighteenth day of Februay A.D. 1869 (signed) Jeremiah BUNCH

107 BOND To WATSON   I John G MITCHELL a Justice of the Peace do hereby Certify that I solemnized the rites of matrimony between John BOND col And Ann WATSON col on the 18 day of February 1869 (signed) John G MITCHELL JP

108 RAWLES To HARRELL I George BISHOP hereby certify that I solemnized the rites of matrimony between James H RAWLES And Clara HARRELL on the ninth day of February AD 1869 (Signed) George BISHOP (JP

109 ASKEW To PUGH   I Bryant LEE a minister of the Gospel do hereby certify that I solemnized the rites of matrimony Between Henry ASKEW And Cloe PUGH on the 6th day of March 1869 (signed) Bryant LEE

110 MITCHELL To JOYNER   I Benj CLARK a minister of the Gospel do hereby certify that I solemnized the rites of matrimony between Abbiat MITCHELL And Mary JOYNER col on the 14th day of March 1869. (signed) Benj CLARK

111 HOLLEY To MEBANE   I A W MEBANE a Justice of the Peace do hereby Certify that I solemnized the rites of matrimony between Ellick HOLLEY col And Mary MEBANE on the Twenty Seventh day of Febry 1869 (signed) A W MEBANE (JP

(10) 144
112 THOMPSON col To TADLOCK   I John G MITCHELL a Justice of the Peace do hereby Certify that I solemnized the rite (sic) of matrimony between Wm S THOMPSON col And Prissilla TADLOCK on the 27th day of February 1869 (Signed) John G MITCHELL JP

113 BOND To RUFFIN   I Abram MEBANE a minister of the Gospel do hereby Certify that I solemnized the rites of matrimony between Miles BOND col And Becky RUFFIN on the 21st day of February 1869 (Signed) Abram MEBANE

114 JERNIGAN To WHITE   I Moses L MIZELL a minister of the Gospel do hereby Certify that I solemnized the rites of matrimony between James R JERNIGAN And Catharine R WHITE on the 21st day of February AD 1869 signed Moses L MIZELL

115 ASKEW To EASON   I John MITCHELL hereby Certify that I Solemnized the rites of matrimony between William W. ASKEW And Amanda EASON on the 25th day of February AD 1869 signed John MITCHELL

116 DUNSTAN To MILLER   I A M CRAIG hereby certify that I solomnized the rites of matrimony between Dr H V DUNSTON And Mary E MILLER on the fifth day of March AD 1869 sgned A. M CRAIG

117 WILNEY To BELL   I Abram MEBANE a minister of the Gospel do hereby Certify that I solemnized the rites of Matrimony between Owen WILNEY col And Pennie BELL col on the Seventh day of March 1869 signed Abram MEBANE

118 BRITTON To NOWELL   I B. B. WILLIAMS hereby certify that I solemnized the rites of matrimony between Daniel W BRITTON and Mary E NOWELL on the 14th day of March AD 1869 (signed) B B WILLIAMS M.G.

119 MIZELL To FLOYD   I George W COBB hereby certify that I solemnized the rites of matrimony between George MIZELL and Ceaney FLOYD on the Eighteenth day of March AD 1869 signed Geo W COBB (JP

1869

(11) 145 Bertie County

120 CASPER To MIZELL I Jeremiah BUNCH (Minister) hereby certify that I solemnized the rites of matrimony between William CASPER and Jane MIZELL on the Eighteenth day of March AD 1869 signed Jeremiah BUNCH

121 GILLAM To BOND I Abram MEBANE a Minister of the Gospel do hereby certify that I solemnized the rites of Matrimony between Frederick GILLAM and rosetta BOND col on the 21st day of March 1869 signed Abram MEBANE

122 LEARRY To OUTLAW I George N GREEN a Justice of the Peace do hereby certify that I solemnized the rites of matrimony between Henry LEARRY and Kattie OUTLAW col on the 23 day of March 1869 signed Geo N GREEN

123 HENDRICKS To BAZEMORE I Bryant LEW a Minister of the Gospel do hereby certify that I solemnized the rites of matrimony between John HENDRICKS and Isabell BAZEMORE on the 25 day of March 1869 (signed) Bryant LEE

124 PITT To BERNARD N C Bertie Co I A M CRAIG hereby certify that I solemnized the rites of matrimony between B F PITT And B W BERNARD on the 24th day of March A D 1869 signed A M CRAIG

125 GARRETT To CHAMBLY State. N.C. Bertie Co I G N GREEN a justice of the Peace hereby certify that I solemnized the rites of matrimony between Abram GARRETT And Cealy A CHAMBLY on the First day of April A D 1869 (signed) G N GREEN J.P.

126 WILLIAMS To WILSON State. N C. Bertie Co. I J W SESSOMS hereby certify that I solemnized the rites of matrimony between Harry WILLIAMS col And Malvina WILSON on the 31st day of March A D 1869 signed John W SESSOMS. J. P.

127 THOMPSON To HODGE State N C Bertie Co. I John G MITCHELL hereby certify that I solemnized the rites of matrimony between George THOMPSON and Margaret HODGE on the 4th day of April A D 1869 (signed) John G MITCHELL (JP

(12) 146
128 HARRISON To DUNDALOW State of N C Bertie Co. I Moses L MIZELL minister of the Gospel hereby certify that I Solemnized the rites of matrimony between Kader HARRISON and Mary DUNDALOW on the first day of April A D 1869 (signed) Moses L MIZELL

129 BELL To CLARK State N C Bertie Co I Benj CLARK a minister of the Gospel hereby certify that that (sic) I solemnized the rites of matrimony between William BELL col And Mouring CLARK on the 4th day of April A D 1869 (signed) Benj CLARK

130 HARRELL To WHITE I a minister of the Gospel hereby certify that I solemnized the rites of matrimony between D C HARRELL And Aritta WHITE on the sixth day of Apil A D 1869 signed Jeremiah BUNCH.

131 CHERRY To SHARP State N C Bertie. I Bryant LEE a minister of the Gospel hereby certify that I solemnized the rites of matrimony between Arter CHERRY and Susan SHARP on the 8th day of April A D 1869 (signed) Bryant Lee

132 HILL To HILL I Abram MEBANE hereby certify that I solemnized the rites of matrimony between James HILL col And Alice HILL col on the 18th day of April A D 1869 (signed) Abram MEBANE

134 (sic) JERNIGAN To BUTLER I Duncan L CALE J. P. hereby certify that I Solemnized the rites of matrimony between Nathaniel JERNIGAN and Victoria BUTLER on the Eleventh day of April A D 1869 (signed) D CALE (JP

135 ACRE To COX I John MITCHELL hereby certify that I solemnized the rites of matrimony between Wm A ACRE and Mary L (or S) COX on the 21st day of April 1869 (signed) John MITCHELL

136 VICK TO BARRETT I R N CROOKS hereby certify that I solemnized the rites of matrimony between Wm H VICK and Ann E BARRETT on the 20th of April A D 1869 signed R N CROOKS RMG

(13) 1467 State of N Carolina Bertie County

1869

137 MYERS To BELL   I John MITCHELL J P hereby certify that I solemnized the rites of matrimony between Isaac MYERS col. and Everline BELL on the 17th day of April A D 69 1869. (signed) John MITCHELL JP

138 WILLIAMS To WILLIAMS I the Rev Benjamin CLARK do hereby certify that I solemnized the rites of Matrimony between Abert WILLIAMS And Rachel WILLIAMS on the Eighteenth day of April A D 1869 (signed) Ben Jamin (sic) CLARK

139 LEE To THOMPSON I Bryant LEE hereby certify that I solemnized the rites of matrimony between Robt LEE col and Bitsy THOMPSON on the 25th day of April A D 1869 (signed) Bryant LEE

140 TADLOCK To CHERRY I Peter MOUNTAIN J. P. hereby certify that I solemnized the rites of matrimony between Peter TADLOCK col and Rose CHERRY col on the 24 day of April A D 1869 signed Peter MOUNTAIN (JP

141 BOWZER To BOND I Peter MOUNTAIN J. P. hereby certify that I Solemnized the rites of matrimony between Henry A BOWZER col And Elizabeth BOND on the 25th day of April A D 1869. (signed) Peter MOUNTAIN (JP

142 JOHNSON To MYERS I Jessee H BUNCH (J.P.) hereby certify that I Solemnized the rites of matrimony between John W JOHNSON And Louisa E MYERS on the 29th day of April A D 1869 signed J H BUNCH (JP

143 CLABON To SMITH I Bryant LEE hereby certify that I solemnized the rites of matrimony between Peter CLABON col and Sopha SMITH col on the 22nd day of May A D 1869 Bryant LEE

(14) 148 State of North Carolina Bertie County
144 WARD To OUTLAW I Henry A BAWGER a Justice of the peace do hereby certify that I solemnized the rites of matrimony between Joseph W WARD col And Joanna OUTLAW col on the 27th day of May A D 1869 Henry A BAWGER (JP

145 HARDY To BISHOP I John MITCHELL hereby certify that I solemnized the rites of matrimony between Joseph H HARDY And Leroy? E BISHOP on the 6th day of May A D 1869 John MITCHELL

146 HARRELL To PEEL I George BISHOP hereby certify that I solemnized the rites of matrimony Between John B HARRELL And Louisa PEEL on the 18th day of May A D 1869 George BISHOP (JP

147 PEELE To BAZEMORE I George BISHOP hereby certify that I solemnized the rites of matrimony between Rubin J PEELE and sarah F BAZEMORE on the 29th day of May A D 1869 George BISHOP (JP

148 LASSITER To STIONS I Jessee H BUNCH (JP) hereby certify that I Solemnized the rites of matrimony between Jessee LASSITER And Elezabeth STIONS on the 23rd day of May A D 1869 Jessee H BUNCH (JP

149 WILLIAMS To CLARK I Benjamon CLARK hereby certify that I solemnized the rites of matrimony between Thomas WILLIAMS col and Chaney CLARK on the 19th day of June A D 1869 Benjamin his X mark CLARK

15=0 MEBANE To HOLLEY I John W SESSOMS here by (sic) certify that I solemnized the rites of matrimony between Joseph MEBANE col. And Ellen HOLLEY on the 23rd day of May A D 1869 John W SESSOMS (JP

151 MILLER To COBB I S T HUGHS hereby certify that I solemnized the rites of matrimony between Frank MILLER and Marina COBB on the 23 day of May A D 1869 S T HUGHES (JP

152 CONNER To POWELL I George BISHOP hereby certify that I Solemnized the rites of matrimony between Joseph CONNER and Kiddy POWELL on the 26 day of May A D 1869 George BISHOP (JP

(15) 149 State of N C Bertie County
153 MIZELL To MILLER I George W COBB a justice of the Peace do hereby certify that I solemnized the rites of matrimony between William MIZELL and Rebecca MILLER on the Twenty-Seventh day of May A D 1869 Gorge W COBB (JP

154 COFFIELD To FREEMAN I George W DOWNING Justice of the Peace hereby certify that I solemnized the rites of matrimony between Ruffin COFFIELD and Martha FREEMAN on the Thirtieth / 30th day of May A D 1869 G W DOWNING (JP

1869

154 (Cont.) Bertie Co N C

155 PEEL To THROWER   I David HARRELL hereby certify that I Solemnized the rites of matrimony between Geo T PEEL And Sarah THROWER on the 29th day of May A D 1869   David HARRELL

156 DUNNING To MORRISS   I a minister of the Gospel do hereby certify that I Solemnized the rites of matrimony between Jessee DUNNING And Nancy E MORRISS on the first day of June A D 1869   Jeremiah BUNCH

157 SMALLWOOD To RUFFIN   I Edward WOOTTEN Presbyter of the P E ch hereby certify that I solemnized the rites of matrimony between J R SMALLWOOD and Annie D RUFFIN on the Tenth day of June A D 1869   Edward WOOTTEN   ch   Rector of St Thomas.

158 PERRY To RAYNER   I Emanuel RAY d'des hereby certify that I solemnized the rites of matrimony between Frank PERRY col and Bettie RAYNER col on the Tenth day of June A D 1869   Emanuel RAY ddes nll? Ch

159 JONES To TAYLOE   I Benjamin CLARK hereby certify that I solemnized the rites of matrimony between Willis JONES and Ruthy TAYLOE on the 19th day of June A D 1869   Benjamin his X mark CLARK

160 WATSON To NICHOLLS   I George BISHOP hereby certify that I solemnized the rites of matrimony between Shadrick WATSON and Bettie NICHOLLS on the 13th day of June A D 1869.   George BISHOP (JP

(18) 150 State of North Carolina Bertie County
161 WATFORD To LASITER   I John W SESSOMS hereby certify that I solemnized the rites of matrimony between William Ben WATFORD and Ida LASSITER on the 19th day of June A D 1869   John W SESSOMS (JP

162 PERRY To WHITE   I John W SESSOMS hereby certify that I solemnized the rites of matrimony between Charles PERRY And Levenia WHITE on the 19th day of June A D 1869   John W SESSOMS JP

163 HOLLEY To LANE   I John W SESSOMS hereby certify that I solemnized the rites of matrimony between Hunter HOLLEY and Easter LANE on the 19th day of June A D 1869   J W SESSOMS (JP

164 MORRISS To BUTLER   I Re E L COX do hereby certify that I solemnized the rites of matrimony between James MORRISS Snr and Nancy E BUTLER on the first day of July A D 1869   Richard E L COX (JP

165 BAKER To BUTLER   I George W COBB hereby certify that I solemnized the rites of matrimony between Wm W BAKER and Judy BUTLER on the 4th day of July A D 1869 George W COBB (JP

166 CHERRY To CHERRY   I Bryant LEE do hereby certify that I solemnized the rites of matrimony between George CHERRY col and Rebecca CHERRY col on the 9th day of July A D 1869   signed   Rev Bryant LEE

167 WATTS To HANCOCK   I George BISHOP hereby certify that I solemnized the rites of matrimony between John WATTS and Harriet HANCOCK on the 18th day of July A D 1869   signed George BISHOP JP

168 BUSH To BISHOP   I George BISHOP hereby certify that I solemnized the rites of matrimony between Robert BUSH and Julia BISHOP on the 18th day of July A D 1869   signed   George BISHOP JP

(17) 151 State of North Carolina Bertie County.
169 SMALLWOOD To PUGH   I Benjamin CLARK hereby certify that I solemnized the rites of matrimony between Benjamin SMALLWOOD and Henrietta PUGH on the First day of August A D 1869   signed Benjamin his X mark CLARK

170 JONES To SLAUGHTER   I James M POWELL hereby certify that I solemnized the rites of matrimony between Simon JONES col and Lidia SLAUGHTER on the 27th day of July A D 1869   signed James M POWELL (JP

171 DEVEREAUX To HILL   I Benjmin CLARK hereby certify that I solemnized the rites of matrimony between Essex DEVEREAUX and Gracy HILL on the 25th day of July A D 1869   signed   Benjamin his X mark CLARK

1869

172 LEARRY To HOLLEY   I John W SESSOMS hereby certify that I solemnized the rites of matrimony between Benja LEARRY and Ferebee HOLLY on the 24th day of July A D 1869   signed   John W SESSOMS (JP

173 GURGANOUS To OUTLAW   I Benjamin CLARK hereby certify that I solemnized the rites of matrimony between Henry S? GURGANOUS col and Lucy OUTLAW on the 27th day of July A D 1869   signed   Benjamin CLARK

174 WILLIAMS To WHEELLER   I Peter MOUNTAIN J P hereby certify that I solemnized the rites of matrimony between Nelson WILLIAMS and Sophia WHEELLER on the 4th day of August A D 1869   Peter MOUNTAIN (JP

175 LEARRY To HARDY   I John W SESSOMS hereby certify that I solemnized the rites of matrimony between Simon LEARRY and Hester HARDY on the 26th day of July A D 1869   signed   John W SESSOMS (JP

176 EVANS To LASSITER   I a minister of the Gospel hereby certify that I Solemnized the rites of matrimony between Aaron J EVANS and Rachel LASSITER on the 12th day of August A D 1869   signed   Jeremiah BUNCH

(18)   152 State of North Carolina Bertie County
177 WALTON To HOGGARD   I George W COBB hereby certify that I solemnized the rites of matrimony between Meridy WALTON and Margaret HOGGARD on the 12th day of August A D 1869   signed   George W COBB (JP

178   PEEL To BROWN   I Peter MOUNTAIN (JP) hereby certify that I Solemnized the rites of matrimony between J T PEEL and Fillis BROWN on the 26th day of August A D 1869   signed   Peter MOUNTAIN (JP

179 ======= SUTTON To REDDITT   I John G MITCHELL a Justice of the Peace hereby Certify that I solemnized the rites of matrimony between Jessee SUTTON And Lucy REDDITT on the 22nd day of August A D 1869 signed John G MITCHELL (JP

180 JOHNSON To THOMPSON   I George BROWN (JP) hereby certify that I solemnized the rites of matrimony between Dallis JOHNSON and Polly THOMPSON on the 29th day of August A D 1869   George BROWN (JP

181   WHITE To COLLINS   I a Minister of the Gospel hereby certify that I solemnized the rites of matrimony between John WHITE and Louisa COLLINS on the sixteenth day of September A D 1869 signed   Jeremiah BUNCH

182 OUTLAW To MITCHELL   I Joseph HOLLAMAN Justice of the Peace hereby certify that I solemnized the rites of matrimony between Britton OUTLAW and Susan C MITCHELL on the 15th day of September A D 1869   Joseph HOLLAMAN JP

183   BERNARD To GRIFFIN   I George BROWN hereby certify that I solemnized the rites of matrimony between Andrew BERNARD and Jane GRIFFIN on the 23 day of September A D 1869   signed   George BROWN JP

184 WALTON To HARDY   I George BISHOP hereby certify that I solemnized the rites of matrimony between David WALTON col and Mary HARDY col on the Sixteenth day of September A D 1869   signed   George BISHOP JP.

(19)   153 State of North Carolina Bertie County
185   MITCHELL To HOLDER   I A M CRAIG hereby certify that I solemnized the rites of matrimony between James E MITCHELL and Eva HOLDER on the nineteenth day of September A D 1869   signed) A M CRAIG MG

186   SUTTON To TADLOCK   I A M CRAIG hereby certify that I solemnized the rites of matrimony between Lewis B SUTTON and Miss Mary C TADLOCK on the 28th day of september A D 1869   signed   A M CRAIG MG.

187   SMITH To MYERS . I Bryant D D (sic) do hereby certify that I solemnized the rites of matrimony between Chas SMITH col and Sallie MYERS col on the 3rd day of October A D 1869   signed   Bryant LEE D D

188 SUTTON To WHITE   I Edward WOOTTEN Minister hereby certify that I solemnized the rites of matrimony between Wm M SUTTON and Martha W WHITE on the Seventh day of October A D 1869   signed   Edward WOOTTEN   Priest of the Holey Catholick Chur (sic)

189 BYRUM To COLLINS   I a minister of the Gospel do hereby certify that I Solemnized the rites of matrimony between

1869

189 (Cont.) James H BYRUM and Elizabeth F COLLINS on the 14th day of October A D 1869   signed   Jeremiah BUNCH

190   JONES To GILLAM   I Peter MOUNTAIN (JP hereby certify that I solemnized the rites of matrimony between Peyton JONES and Harriet GILLAM on the (blank) day of A D 1869 (sic)   signed   Peter MOUNTAIN JP

191   SESSOMS To BEASLY   I John MITCHELL hereby certify that I solemnized the rites of matrimony between Preston H SESSOMS and Annie E. BEASLY on the 3rd day of Nove (sic) A D 1869 signed   John MITCHELL

192   WHITE To NIXON   I Moses L MIZELL a minister of the Gospel do hereby certify that I solemnized the rites of matrimony between Manassa WHITE and Mary E NIXON on the Twenty-First day of October A D 1869   signed   Moses L MIZELL

(20)   154   State of North Carolina Bertie County
193   LAW To HOLLEY   I Abram MEBANE hereby certify that I solemnized the rites of matrimony between Lazarus LAW and Susan HOLLEY on the Twenty-Fourth day of October A D 1869   signed   Abram MEBANE Minister

194   MORRISS To PERRY   I B B WILLIAMS mist (sic) of Gospel hereby certify that I solemnized the rites of Matrimony between M B MORRISS and Margaret A PERRY on the 4th day of November A D 1869   signed   B B WILLIAMS

195   CASPER To JENKINS   I Bryant LEE D D do hereby certify that I solemnized the rites of matrimony between Arter CASPER col And Frances JENKINS col on the 7th day of Novemer A D 1869   signed   Bryant LEE D D

196   BIRD To WHITAKER   I a minister of the Gospel do hereby certify that I Solemnized the rites of Matrimony between Wm G BIRD and Mrs. Mary E WHITAKER on the Eleventh day of November A D 1869   signed   Jeremiah BUNCH

197   RUFFIN To WILLIAMS   I Geo W DOWNING J P hereby certify that I solemnized the rites of matrimony between Minor RUFFIN and Mary WILLIAMS col on the Sixteenth day of November A D 1869   signed   Geo W DOWNING. JP.

198   WYNN To FREEMAN   I Emanuel REYNOLD a Minister of the Gospel hereby certify that I solemnized the rites of matrimony between Granville WYNN col and Mariah FREEMAN on the Fourteenth day of November A D 1869   signed   Emanuel REYNOLD

199   JONES To BOND   I Peter MOUNTAIN .JP. hereby certify that I solemnized the rites of matrimony between Eli   JONES col and Katie BOND col on the 18th day of November A D 1869   signed   Peter MOUNTAIN JP

200   SPIVEY To TAYLOE   I Peter MOUNTAIN JP hereby certify that I solemnized the rites of matrimony between George SPIVEY col and Amanda TAYLOE col on the 19th day of November A D 1869   signed   Peter MOUNTAIN JP

(21)   155   State of North Carolina Bertie County
201   SESSOMS To PERRY   I John MITCHELL hereby certify that I solemnized the rites of Matrimony between D V SESSOMS Jr and Martha PERRY on the 24th day of November A D 1869   signed   John MITCHELL JP

202   MITCHELL To HOGGARD   I Thomas HOGGARD hereby certify that I solemnized the rites of Matrimony between Rufus MITCHELL and Penelope HOGGARD on the 22nd day of November A D 1869   signed   Thos HOGGARD

203   BRITTON To RICE   I Geo W DOWNING JP hereby certify that I solemnized the rites of matrimony between Auntny? L BRITTON col and Hettie RICE col on the twentieth day of November A D 1869   signed   Geo W DOWNING JP

204   BASNETT To DEAM   I Abram MAVIN hereby certify that I solemnized the rites of matrimony between Thomas BASNETT And Mariah DEAM on the 21st day of November A D 1869   signed   Abram MABIN, MG

205   CLARK To RUFFIN   I George BROWN hereby certify that I solemnized the rites of matrimony between George CLARK col And Winnie RUFFIN on the 2nd day of November December A D 1869   signed   George BROWN JP

206   BARRETT To SKIRVIN   I R N CROOKS hereby Certify that I solemnized the rites of matrimony between M E G BARRETT and Susan C SKIRVIN on the Seventh day of December A D 1869   signed   R N CROOKS MG

1869

207 WILLIAMS To WILLIAMS I George BROWN hereby certify that I solemnized the rites of matrimony between Hampton WILLIAMS and Marenda WILLIAMS on the 12th day of December A D 1869 signed George BROWN JP

208 WILLIAMS To HARGROVE I Bryant LEE D D do hereby certify that I solemnized the rites of matrimony between Nelson WILLIAMS And Fanny HARGROVE on the 10th day of December A D 1869 signed Bryant LEE D D

(22) 156 State of North Carolina Bertie County
209 DOWNING To BRITT I Edward WOOTTEN (Priest) hereby certify that I Solemnized the rites of matrimony between George W DOWNING and Adeline P BRITT on the ninth day of Februay A D 1869 signed Edward WOOTTEN Rector of St Thomas Church

210 WILLIAMS To MIZELL I A M CRAIG hereby certify that I solemnized the rites of Matrimony between Docton WILLIAMS And Sallie MIZELL on the Twelfth day of December A D 1869 signed A M CRAIG MG.

211 BROWN To PITMAN I a minister of the Gospel hereby certify that I Solemnized the rites of matrimony between Robert R. BROWN and Virginia C PITMAN on the 16th day of December A D 1869 signed Jeremiah BUNCH

212 DAVIDSON To DUNNING I Thos HOGGARD hereby certify that I solemnized the rites of matrimony between George M DAVIDSON and Mary E DUNNING on the 19th day of December A D 1869 signed Thos HOGGARD

213 WILLOUGHBY To CHERRY I John MITCHELL hereby certify that I solemnized the rites of matrimony between Spencer WILLOUGHBY and Caroline CHERRY on the 16th day of Decem (sic) A D 1869 signed John MITCHELL

214 SMALLWOOD To HARDY I Peter MOUNTAIN, J P. hereby certify that I solemnized the rites of matrimony between Noah SMALLWOOD and Mary Ann HARDY on the 18th day of December A D 1869 signed Peter MOUNTAIN JP

215 LEE To SMALLWOOD I M C RHODES hereby certify that I solemnized the rites of matrimony between Moses LEE col and Lizina SMALLWOOD on the 16th day of December A D 1869 signed M C RHODES

216 JACOCKS To NICHOLLS I Edward WOOTTEN a Presbyter of the P E (sic) Church herey certify that I solemnized the rites of matrimony between Jonathan J JACOCKS and Emily B NICHOLLS on the Twenty first day of December A D 1869 signed Edward WOOTTEN Rector of St Thomas Church

(23) 157 State of North Carolina Bertie County
217 LUCESTER To RAY I J W SMITH hereby certify that I solemnized the rites of matrimony between Jonathan LUCESTER and Jane RAY on the 23rd day of Decembr A D 1869 signed J W SMITH JP

218 SMITH To BEASLY I Emanuel REYNOLD a minister Gospel (sic) hereby certify that I solemnized the rites of matrimony between Stephen SMITH and Mariah BEASLY on the Twenty First Day of December AD 1869 signed Emanuel REYNOLDS

219 PERRY To HUGHES I George W COBB hereby certify that I solemnized the rites of matrimony between William W PERRY and Celia T HUGHES on the 23rd day of December A D 1869 signed George W COBB (JP)

220 LEE TO PIERCE I Bryant LEE D D do hereby certify that I solemnized the rites of matrimony between Anthony LEE and Jennett PEARCE on the 23 day of December A D 1869 signed Bryant LEE DD

221 BOON To HARDY I John W SESSOMS hereby certify that I solemnized the rites of matrimony between Harry BOON and Hulday HARDY col on the 24th day of December AD 1869 signed John W SESSOMS JP

222 WHITE To BENNETT I John W SESSOMS hereby certify that I solemnized the rites of matrimony between Haywood WHITE and Marinda BENNETT on the 24th day of December AD 1869 signed John W SESSOMS JP

223 PUGH To BOND I Peter MOUNTAIN .J P. hereby certify that I solemnized the rites of matrimony between David PUGH and Penny BOND on the 24th day of December AD 1869 signed Peter MOUNTAIN JP

1870

224 BAZEMORE To CASPER I Bryant LEE D D hereby certify that I solemnized the rites of Matrimony between Peter F. BAZEMORE and Harriett CASPER on the 25th day of December AD 1869 signed Bryant LEE DD

(24) 158 State of North Carolina Bertie County
225 CHERRY To GILLAM I John MITCHELL hereby certify that I solemnized the rites of matrimony between Wright CHERRY and Malinda GILLAM on the 29th day of Decembr AD 1869 signed John MITCHELL

226 BOND To SMITHWICK I Peter MOUNTAIN JP hereby certify that I solemnized the rites of matrimony between Bob BOND and Delila SMITHWICK on the 24th day of December A D 1869 signed Beter MOUNTAIN JP

227 WYNNS To WHITE I B B WILLIAMS minister Gospel (sic) hereby certify that I solemnized the rites of matrimony between York WYNNS And Susan? WHITE on the 27th day of December AD 1869 signed B B WILLIAMS

228 GILLAM To SMALLWOOD I Abram MABIN here by (sic) certify that I solemnized the rites of matrimony between Willis GILLAM and Tempy SMALLWOOD on the 20th day of march A D 186970 signed Abram MABIN M of G

229 LAWRENCE To MORRISS I J W SMITH hereby certify that I solemnized the rites of matrimony between Jeremiah ===== LAWRENCE col and Ara E MORRISS on the 28th day of December A D 1869 signed J W SMITH JP

230 BONNER To NICHOLLS I Thadeous WILSON hereby certify that I solemnized the rites of matrimony between Thomas BONNER and Lucy NICHOLLS on the 30th day of December AD 1869 signed Thadeous WILSON

231 SESSOMS To MORRISS I Geo N GREEN hereby certify that I solemnized the rites of matrimony between Tony SESSOMS and Hester MORRISS on the 30th day of December AD 1869 signed Geo N GREEN JP

232 WHITE To WHITE I S T HUGHES hereby certify that I solemnized the rites of matrimony between Arter WHITE and Jane WHITE on the 1st day of January AD 18670 signed S T. HUGHES (JP

(25) 159 State of North Carolina Bertie County
233 WATFORD To MORING I John G MITCHELL hereby certify that I solemnized the rites of matrimony between Henry WATFORD and Jane MORING on the 30th day of December A D 1869 signed John G MITCHELL JP

234 WHITE To BRYANT I Moses L MIZELL minister of the Gospel hereby certify that I solemnized the rites of matrimony between Watson L WHITE and Nancy BRYANT on the Fifth day of January A D 1870 signed Moses L MIZELL

235 RANKINS To JACKSON I Thadeous WILSON hereby certify that I solemnized the rites of matrimony between Jordan RANKINS and Caroline JACKSON on the 6th day of January A D 1870 signed Thadeous WILSON

236 HOGGARD To BUTT I Bryant LEE D.D. do hereby certify that I solemnized the rites of matrimony between John D HOGGARD col and Francis A BUTT on the 6th day of January A D 18670 signed Bryant LEE D D

237 BUNCH To CASPER I Bryant LEE D D do hereby certify that I solemnized the rites of matrimony between Henry BUNCH and Jane CASPER on the 13th day of January A D 1870 signed Bryant LEE D D

238 JERNIGAN To BANZORA (sic) I Moses L MIZELL Minister of the Gospel hereby certify that I solemnized the rites of matrimony between Starkey JERNIGAN and Banzora MYERS on the Tweltfeh day of January A D 1870 signed Moses L MIZELL

239 TREADWELL To MORRISS I Thadeous WILSON hereby certify that I solemnized the rites of matrimony between Drew TREDWELL and Emaline MORRISS col on the 19th day of Janry (sic) A D 1870 signed Thadeous WILSON

240 BAZEMOR (sic) To TODD I a minister of the Gospel hereby certify that I solemnized the rites of matrimony between James G BAZEMORE and Nancy TODD on the Twenty-Seventh day of January A D 1870 signed Jeremiah BUNCH

(26) 160 State of North Carolina Bertie County

1870

241 BOND To BOND I Peter MOUNTAIN JP hereby certify that I solemnized the rites of matrimony between Washington BOND and Susan BOND on the 5th day of February A D 1870 signed Peter MOUNTAIN JP

242 BROWN To FREEMAN I Richard E L COX hereby certify that I solemnized the rites of matrimony between George BROWN and Rachel FREEMAN on the 22nd day of January AD 1870 signed Richard E L COX JP

243 EVANS To ETHERIDGE I Emanul REYNOLDS Minister Gospel (sic) hereby certify that I solemnized the rites of matrimony between Ishniel? EVANS and Morin ETHERIDGE on the 10th day of January A D 1870 signed Emanuel REYNOLDS M.G.

244 BROWN To PEARCE I B B WILLIAMS ninst Gospel hereby certify that I Solemnized the rites of matrimony between Henderson BROWN and Mary A PEARCE on the 6th day of Jany A D 1870 signed B B WILLIAMS

245 MIZELL To WHITE I John W SESSOMS hereby certify that I solemnized the rites of matrimony between Mathew H MIZELL and Amanda WHITE on the 6th day of January A D 1870 signed J W SESSOMS JP

246 RICE To TAYLOE I Peter MOUNTAN hereby certify that I solemnized the rites of matrimony between Daniel RICE and Nancy TAYLOE on the 8th day of January AD 1870 signed Peter MOUNTAIN JP

247 WILLIAMS To RAYNER I Geo W COBB a justice of the Peace hereby certify that I solemnized the rites of matrimony between Vanburin WILLIAMS and Kary RAYNER on the ninth day of January AD 1870 (signed) Geo W COBB JP

248 BROWN To WEST I Thad WILSON do hereby certify that I solemnized the rites of matrimony between James BROWN and Mary WEST on the 2nd day of January A D 1870 signed Thad WILSON

(27) 161 State of North Carolina Bertie County
249 SPRUILL To CAPEHART I R N CROOKS hereby certify that I solemnized the rites of matrimony between J R H SPRUILL and S E CAPEHART on the 23rd day of January AD 18670 signed R N CROOKS M G

250 ASKEW To BACKUS I John MITCHELL hereby certify that I solemnized the rites of matrimony between William P ASKEW and Penicy? BACKUS on the 23 day of January A D 1870 signed John MITCHELL

251 WILLIAMS To WILLIAMS I Gorge BROWN do hereby certify that I solemnized the rites of matrimony between Soloman WILLIAMS and Julia WILLIAMS on the 22 day of Janeay A D 1870 signed George BROWN JP

252 THOMPSON To TAYLOE I Gorge BROWN hereby certify that I solemnized the rites of matrimony between Nelson THOMPSON And Betsy TAYLOE on the 7th day of February AD 1870 signed Geo BROWN JP

253 PUGH To WILLIAMS I Benjamin CLARK hereby certify that I solemnized the rites of matrimony between Daniel PUGH col and Rose WILLIAMS on the 27th day of January A D 1870 signed) Benjamin CLARK Rev

254 SPELLER To WARD I Peter MOUNTAIN JP hereby certify that I solemnized the rites of matrimony between Rubin SPELLER and Emily WARD on the 3rd day of february A D 1870 signed Peter MOUNTAIN JP

255 COGGINS To LYNCH I Peter MOUNTAIN JP hereby certify that I Solemnized the rites of matrimony between Robert COGGINS and Francis LYNCH on the 17th day of February A D 1870 signed Peter MOUNTAIN JP

256 BAKER To BIRD I John W SESSOMS hereby certify that I solemnized the rites of matrimony between George BAKER and Celia E BIRD on the 6th day of February A D 1870 signed J W SESSOMS JP

(28) 162 State of North Carolina Bertie County
257 BOND To RUFFIN I Abram MEBIN hereby certify that I solemnized the rites of matrimony between Joseph BOND and Winnie RUFFIN on the 20th day of Feby A D 1870 signed Abram MABIN MG

258 BRIGGS To RUFFIN I George BROWN hereby certify that I solemnized the rites of matrimony between Willis BRIGGS And Phillis RUFFIN on the 5th day of February AD 1870 signed George BROWN JP

1870

259 PEELE To MORRISS   I B B WILLIAMS hereby certify that I solemnized the rites of matrimony between Drew PEELE and Mary E MORRISS on the Eighth day of February A D 1870   signed   B B WILLIAMS MG

260 ASKEW To CHERRY   I John MITCHELL hereby certify that I solemnized the rites of matrimony between Aaron O ASKEW and Jane O CHERRY on the 10th day of Februay A D 1870   signed   John MITCHELL

261 GRAY To BOND   I Peter MOUNTAIN JP hereby certify that I solemnized the rites of matrimony between Benjamin GRAY col and Margaret BOND on the 17th day of Februay AD 1870   signed   Peter MOUNTAIN JP

262 BOND To GILLAM   I M C RHODES hereby certify that I solemnized the rites of matrimony between Abram BOND col and Harriet GILLAM on the 19th day of Febry A D 1870   signed   M C RHODES

263 EURE To DUNNING   I John MITCHELL hereby certify that I Solemnized the rites of matrimony between Mills EURE and Laura J DUNNING on th (sic) 13th day of Februay AD 1870   signed   John MITCHELL

264 SMALLWOOD To BOND   I Abram MABIN hereby certify that I solemnized the rites of matrimony between Solomon SMALL-WOOD and Caroline BOND on the 20th day of Feby A D 1870   signed   Abram MABIN MG

(29) 163 State of North Carolina Bertie County
265 STONE To MURRA   I a mnister of the Gospel hereby certify that I solemnized the rites of matrimony between   John STONE and Annie MURRA on the 17th day of Februay AD 1870   signed   Jeremiah BUNCH

266 ASKEW To CHERRY   I John MITCHELL hereby certify that I solemnized the rites of matrimony between Thos ASKEW col and Becka CHERRY on the 24th day of February AD 1870   signed   John MITCHELL

267   BUTLER To WHITE   I Moses L MIZELL minister of the Gospel hereby certify that I solemnized the rites of matrimony between Harvey BUTLER And Marinah WHITE on the 21st day of Februy AD 1870   signed   Moses L MIZELL

268 PEEBLES To POWELL   I Bryant LEE D D hereby certify that I solemnized the rites of matrimony between Peter PEEBLES col and Clara POWELL on the 25th day of Feby AD 1870   signed   Bryant LEE D D

269   SCOTT To RASCOE   I M C RHODES hereby certify that I solemnized the rites of matrimony between Cater SCOTT col and Harriet RASCOE on the 7th day of March AD 1870   signed   M C RHODES

270 HOLLEY To SUTTON   I Thad WILSON do hereby Certify that I solemnized the rites of matrimoy between Nead HOLLEY col and Luvine? SUTTON on the 6th day of March AD 18670 signed   Thad WILSON

271 LEE To SPIVEY   I Bryant LEE D D do hereby certify that I solemnized the rites of matrimony between Jack LEE and Matilda SPIVEY on the 6th day of March AD 1870   signed   Bryant LEE D D

272 THOMPSON To SMALLWOOD   I George BROW (sic) do hereby certify that I solemnized the rites of matrimony between Worter THOMPSON   and Anica SMALLWOOD on the 10th day of March AD 1870   signed   George BROWN JP

(30) 164 State of North Carolina Bertie County
273   GILLAM To GILLAM   I Peter MOUNTAIN hereby certify that I solemnized the rites of matrimony between Armistead GILLAM And Celia GILLAM on the 26th day of March AD 1870   signed   Peter MOUNTAIN JP

274 RASCOE To SHIELDS   I Abram MABIN hereby certify that I solemnized the rites of matrimony between Britton RASCOE Affa Abba SHIELDS (sic) on the 20th day of March AD 1870   signed   Abram MABIN MG

275   ODOM To RUFFIN   I Geo W DOWNING J P hereby certify that I solemnized the rites of matrimony between Isum ODOM and Dolly RUFFIN on the ninteenth day of March AD 1870   signed   Geo W DOWNING JP

276   MC DERMITT To CONNER   I George W DOWNING Justice of the Peace hereby certify that I Solemnized the rites of matrimony between Jessee MC DERMITT And Elizabeth CONNER on the 8th day of March A D 1870   signed   Geo W DOWNING JP

1870

277 FREEMAN To CHERRY I Bryant LEE D D do hereby certify that I solemnized the rites of matrimony between Ned FREEMAN and Tempy CHERRY on the 10th day of March A D 1870 signed Bryant LEE D D

278 MANNING To DAVIS I George BROWN do hereby certify that I solemnized the rites of matrimony between Joseph MANNING and Levinia DAVIS col on the 12th day of March AD 1870 signed Geo BROWN JP

279 WHITE To WHITE I manuel REYNOLDS Minister hereby certify that I Solemnized the rites of matrimony between Ben WHITE and Ann WHITE on the 12th day of March AD 1870 signed Imanuel REYNOLDS

280 MIZELL To ASBEL I David HARRELL hereby certify that I solemnized the rites of matrimony between Thadeus MIZELL and Marinda A ASBEL on the 10th day of March A D 1870 signed David HARRELL

(31) 165 State of North Carolina Bertie County
281 MIZELL To WILLIFORD I David HARRELL do hereby certify that I solemnized the rites of Matrimony between Starkey E MIZELL and Jarsey WILLIFORD on the 13th day of March AD 1870 signed David HARRELL

282 SIMMONS To THOMPSON I Bryant LEE D D do hereby certify that I solemnized the rites of Matrimony between Ceaser SIMMONS and Lizina THOMPSON on the 13th day of March AD 1870 signed Bryant LEE D D

283 CLARK To BROWN I George BROWN do hereby certify that I solemnized the rites of matrimony between Harry CLARK And Agness BROWN on the 13th day of March AD 1870 signed Geo BROWN JP

284 TAYLOE To TODD I Bryant LEE D D do hereby certify that I solemnized the rites of matrimony between Aquilla TAYLOE and Josephine TODD on the 17th day of March AD 1870 signed Bryant LEE D D

285 COOPER To WEST I Peter MOUNTAIN J P hereby certify that I Solemnized the rites of matrimony between George COOPER And Penic?y WEST on the 19th day of March AD 1870 signed Peter MOUNTAIN J P

286 PARKER To BAZEMORE I a minister of the Gospel hereby certify that I solemnized the rites of matrimony between James B PARKER And Mary E BAZEMORE on the Twenty fourth day of March AD 1870 signed Jeremiah BUNCH

287 EPPS To WILLIAMS I Rev Ben CLARK do hereby certify that I solemnized the rites of Matrimony between Harry EPPS and Emaline WILLIAMS col on the 26th day of March A D 1870 signed Rev Ben CLARK

288 WHITE To WHITE I Thos HOGGARD hereby Certify that I solemnized the rites of matrimony between Kenneth WHITE and Martha J WHITE on the 27th day of March AD 1870 signed Thos HOGGARD

(32) 166 State of North Carolina Bertie County
289 BUNCH To WARD I a minister of the Gospel hereby certify that I solemni___ the rites of matrimony between Wm H BUNCH and Henrietta WARD on the seventh day of April AD 1870 signed Jeremiah BUNCH

290 EVERETT To PUGH I George BROWN do hereby certify that I solemnized the rites of matrimony between Zarra EVERETT And Hasty PUGH on the 10th day of April AD 1870 signed George BROWN J P

291 GRAY To RHODES I Henry C COOPER JP hereby certify that I solemnized the rites of matrimony between Maderson GRAY and Mariah RHODES on the 7th day of April AD 1870 signed Henry C COOPER JP

292 BAZEMORE To RUFFIN I Bryant LEE DD do hereby certify that I solemnized the rites of matrimony between Nelson BAZEMORE And Chaney RUFFIN on the 7th day of April AD 1870 signed Bryant LEE D D

293 WATFORD To WILSON I Immanuel REYNOLDS Minister hereby certify that I Solemnized the rites of matrimony between Daniel WATFORD col and Ellen WILSON col on the 10th day of April AD 1870 signed Immanuel REYNOLDS

294 ELLYSON To BENNETT I Immanuel REYNOLDS minister hereby certify that I Solemnized the rites of matrimony between Washington ELLYSON col And Esther BENNETT on the Tenth day of April AD 1870 signed Immanuel REYNOLDS

1870

295 PRITCHARD To BAZEMORE I a minister of the Gospel hereby certify that I Solemnized the rites of matrimony bettween A J PRITCHARD and Sallie Ann BAZEMORE on the 10th day of April AD 1870 signed Jeremiah BUNCH

296 MYERS To MORRIS I John MITCHELL hereby certify that I solemnized the rites of matrimony between Ralph MYERS and Emiline MORRIS on the 12th day of April AD 1870 signed John MITCHELL

(33) 167 State of North Carolina Bertie County
297 CHERRY To OUTLAW I Edward WOOTTEN Priest P E Church hereby certify that I solemnized the rites of matrimony between Henry CHERRY and Milly OUTLAW on the 14th day of April A D 1870 signed Edwootten Priest in the P E/church

298 RHODES To CAPEHART I R N CROOKS Regular Minister of the Gospel hereby certify that I solemnized the rites of Matrimony between Thomas J RHODES and Mary E CAPEHART on the Twenty First day of April AD 1870 signed R N CROOKS R M G

299 MITCHELL To RUFFIN I John MITCHELL hereby certify that I solemnized the rites of matrimony between F V MITCHELL And Susan RUFFIN on the 21st day of April AD 1870 signed John MITCHELL

300 CLARK To WALTON I George BROWN do hereby certify that I solemnized the rites of matrimony between Frank CLARK col and Judy WALTON col on the 29th day of April A D 1870 signed. George BROWN J P

301 BOND To CLARK I George BROWN do hereby certify that I Solemnized the rites of matrimony between Thomas BOND col and Annice CLARK col on the 29th day of April A D 1870 signed George BROWN J P

302 PAGE To WILLIAMS I George BROWN do hereby certify that I solemnized the rites of matrimony between George PAGE col and Cherry WILLIAMS col on the 1st day of May AD 1870 signed George BROWN J P

303 FIELDS To WILLIAMS I George BROWN do hereby certify that I Solemnized the rites of matrimony between Andrew FIELDS col and Sallie WILLIAMS on the 1st day of May AD 1870 Signed George BROWN J P

304 BURDEN To CHERRY I Bryant LEE D D hereby certify that I solemnized the rites of matrimony between Madison BURDEN col and Sarah CHERRY col on the 28th day of April A D 1870 signed Bryant LEE D D

(34) 168 State of North Carolina Bertie County
305 304 THOMPSON To SUTTON I George BROWN do hereby certify that I Solemnized the rites of matrimoney between Hampton THOMPSON And Nelly SUTTON col on the 7th day of May AD 1870 signed George BROWN JP

306 305 SMALLWOOD To SMALLWOOD I M C RHODES hereby certify that I solemnized the rites of matrimony between Prince SMALLWOOD col and Lurinda SMALLWOOD col on the 30th day of April AD 1870 signed M C RHODES Bap Mins

307 MITCHELL To HYMAN I John G MITCHELL do hereby certify that I solemnized the rites of matrimony between George MITCHELL and Josephine HYMAN on the 5th day of May AD 1870 signed John G MITCHELL JP

308 HOWELL To WILLIAMS I George BROWN do hereby certify that I solemnized the rites of matrimony between Henry W HOWELL col and Emaline WILLIAMS on the 7th day of May AD 1870 signed George BROWN JP

309 PAGE To MIZELL I a minister of the Gospel hereby certify that I solemnized the rites of matrimony between Soloman PAGE and Rebecca MIZELL on the Eight (sic) day of May AD 1870 signed Jeremiah BUNCH

310 BAZEMORE To SHARROCK I Bryant LEE DD hereby certify that I solemnized the rites of matrimony between Winston BAZEMORE and Delia SHARROCK on the 10th day of May AD 1870 signed Bryant LEE DD

311 BRIDGER To BAZEMORE I Bryant LEE DD hereby certify that I solemnized the rites of matrimony between Justin BRIDGER and Isabella BAZEMORE on the 12th day of May AD 1870 signed Bryant LEE

312 BOND To CHERRY I Peter MOUNTAIN J P hereby certify that I solemnized the rites of matrimony between Stewart

1870

312 (Cont.) BOND and Ester CHERRY col on the 11th day of May AD 1870 signed Peter MOUNTAIN J P

(35) 169 State of North Carolina Bertie County
313 THOMPSON To PUGH I George BROWN hereby certify that I Solemnized the rites of matrimony between Friley? THOMP-
SON and Edie PUGH on the 15th day of May AD 1870 signed George BROWN

314 BOND To WORLEY I Rev Abram NABIN hereby certify that I solemnized the rites of matrimony between Neptan BOND and Chaney WORLEY col on the 14th day of May AD 1870 signed Abram NABIN

315 PIERCE To PATTERSON I Edward PIERCE hereby certify that I solemnized the rites of matrimony bettween James K PIERCE and Mary PATTERSON on the 19th day of May AD 1870 signed Edward PIEARCE

316 BISHOP To RUFFIN I George BROWN do hereby certify that I solemnized the rites of matrimony between Richard BISHOP and Rosetta RUFFIN col on the 29th day of May AD 1870 signed George BROWN J P

317 HOWARD To PARKER I a minister of the Gospel hereby certify that I solemnized the rites of matrimony between Reddick H HOWARD and Parthena M PARKER on the 22 day of May A D 1870 signed Jeremiah BUNCH

318 SLURGE To MC GLAUHON I S T HUGHES hereby certify that I solemnized the rites of Matrimony between Harry SLURGE and Marinda MC GLAUHON on the 22nd day of May AD 1870 signed S T HUGHES

319 ====== DANALDS BUNCH (sic) I J W SMITH hereby certify that I Solemnized the rites of Matrimony between Giles DONALD and Bitsy BUNCH on the 26th day of AD 1870 (sic) signed J W SMITH JP

320 ANDERSON To POWELL I George BROWN do hereby certify that I Solemnized the rites of matrimony between Henry ANDERSON col and Amand (sic) POWELL on the 28th day of May AD 1870 signed Geo BROWN J P

(36) 170 State of North Carolina Bertie County
321 WILSON To JONES I S T HUGHES hereby certify that I solemnized the rites of matrimony between Thomas WILSON col and Patsey JONES col on the Twenty ninth day of May AD 1870 signed S T HUGHES

322 ===== STEWART To WYNN I John G MITCHELL hereby certify that I solemnized the rites of matrimony between Charles STEWART and Annie M WYNNE on the 28th day of May AD 1870 signed John G MITCHELL JP

323 PRITCHARD To BUTLER I a mnister of the Gospel hereby certify that I solemnized the rites of matrimony between Docton PRITCHARD and Martha C BUTLER on the Second day of June AD 1870 signed Jeremiah BUNCH

324 LEE To PHELPS I Rev Ben CLARK hereby certify that I solemnized the rites of matrimony between George W LEE col and Henrietta PHELPS col on the 5th day of June AD 1870 signed Rev Ben CLARK

325 COOPER To HOGGARD I Henry C COOPER J P hereby certify that I solemnized the rites of matrimony between Haywood COOPER and Annice HOGGARD on the 5th day of June AD 1870 signed Henry C COOPER JP

326 SAVAGE To FRANCIS I Peter MOUNTAIN J P hereby certify that I solemnized the rites of matrimony between Henry SAVAGE Isabella A FRANCIS (sic) col on the 9th day of June AD 1870 signed Peter MOUNTAIN JP

327 LEE To BOND I Peter MOUNTAIN J P hereby certify that I solemnized the rites of matrimony between John LEE col and Henrietta BOND col on the 9th day of June AD 1870 [End of entry.]

328 BUNCH TO MC FARLAND I B B WILLIAMS hereby certify that I solemnized the rites of matrimony between James BUNCH and Mary MC FARLAND on the 12th day of June AD 1870 signed B B WILLIAMS M G

(37) 171 State of North Carolina Bertie County
329 HENRY To WHITE I S T HUGHES hereby certify that I solemnized the rites of matrimony between Reddick HENRY and Eliza WHITE on the 11th day of June AD 1870 signed S T HUGHES JP

1870

330   MIZELL To HOLLEY   I John W SESSOMS (JP) hereby certify that I solemnized the rites of matrimony between John MIZELL col and Fanny HOLLEY col on the Eighteenth day of June AD 1870   signed   John W SESSOMS JP

331   BAZEMORE To FREEMAN   I Bryant LEE D D hereby certify chat I solemnized the rites of matrimony between James R BAZEMORE col and Nancy FREEMAN on the 18th day of June 1870   signed   Bryant LEE

332   HARRELL To REDDICK   I Henry C COOPER hereby certify that I solemnized the rites of matrimony between Antony HARRELL col And Mollie REDDICK col on the 19th day of April AD 1870   signed   H C COOPER J P

333   ASKEW To WEBB   I Edward WOOTTEN Priest of the P E Ch hereby certify that I solemnized the rites of matrimony between Richard W ASKEW And Elizabeth WEBB on the 15th day of June AD 1870   signed   Edward WOOTTEN Priest of P S? ch Rector St Thomas church

334   MORING To COOPER   I John G MITCHELL J P hereby certify that I solemnized the rites of matrimony between Joseph MORING and Henrietha COOPER col on the 18th day of June AD 1870   signed   John G MITCHELL JP

335   RAYNER To MOORE   I Rev Abram NAVIN hereby certify that I solemnized the rites of matrimony between Noah RAYNER col and Sallie MOORE on the 18th day of June AD 1870   signed   Abram NABIN

336   WILLIAMS To COBB   I Geo W COBB hereby certify that I solemnized the rites of matrimony between Charles H WILLIAMS and Ceneth P COBB on the 26th day of June A D 1870   signed   Geo W COBB JP

(38)   172   State of North Carolina Bertie County
337   WILSON To LANE   I Emanuel REYNOLDS minister hereby certify that I solemnized the rites of matrimony between Andrew WILSON and Sara LANE col on the 26th day of June AD 1870   signed   Emanuel REYNOLDS

338   HARE To FREEMAN   I John W SESSOMS hereby certify that I solemnized the rites of matrimony between Starkey HARE And Martha FREEMAN on the 25th day of June AD 1870   signed   John W SESSOMS JP

339   ALEN To HECKSTALL   I John G MITCHELL J P hereby certify that I solemnized the rites of matrimony between ALEN col (sic) and Jane HECKSTALL col on the 12th day of July AD 1870   signed   John G MITCHELL J P

340   BELL To CLARK   I George BROWN do hereby certify that I solemnized the rites of matrimony between William BELL col and Lidia CLARK on the 18th day of July AD 1870   signed   George BROWN J P

341   BRYANT To HOLLEY   I Geo W COBB hereby certify that I solemnized the rites of matrimony between Alfred BRYANT col and Patsey HOLLEY col on the 24th day of July AD 1870   signed   Geo W COBB (JP)

342   BYRUM To MITCHELL   I B B WILLIAMS hereby certify that I solemnized the rites of matrimony between Daniel E BYRUM and Alice A MITCHELL on the 21st day of July AD 1870   signed   B B WILLIAMS MG

344 (sic)   WINTON To COSTAN   I Bryant LEE D D hereby certify that I solemnized the rites of matrimony between Robert WINTON and Sallie COSTAN on the Eleventh day of August A D 1870   signed   Bryant LEE

345   POWELL To WIGGINS   I George BROWN do hereby certify that I solemnized the rites of Matrimony between Lewis POWELL col and Tempy WIGGINS on the 15th day of August A D 1870   signed   Geo BROWN J P

(39)   173   State of North Carolina Bertie County
346   LAWRENCE To BUTLER   I Moses L MIZELL mnister of the Gospel hereby certify that I solemnized the rites of matrimony between Robert LAWRENCE And Margaret BUTLER on the on the (sic) sixteenth day of August AD 1870   signed   Moses L MIZELL

347   MORRISS To JERNIGAN   I aminister of the Gospel hereby certify that I solemnized the rites of matrimony between Allen MORRISS and Sarah JERNIGAN on the first day of first day of (sic) September A D 1870   signed   Jeremiah BUNCH

1870

348 JACKSON To BOYKIN   I Bryant LEE D D hereby certify that I solemnized the rites of matrimony between Thomas J JACKSON and Harriet E BOYKIN on the 8th day of september AD 1870 signed Bryant LEE

349 OUTLAW To ASKEW   I Edward WOOTTEN Priest of The PE ch hereby certify that I solemnized the rites of matrimony between Oscar ====== OUTLAW col And Rose ASKEW col on the Thirteenth day of August AD 1870 signed Edward WOOTTEN Rector of St Thomas ch Windsor

350 RUFFIN To THOMAS   I George W DOWNING J P hereby certify that I solemnized the rites of matrimony between Noah RUFFIN col and Patsey THOMAS col on the Twenty fifth day of August AD. 1870   signed Geo W DOWNING JP Bertie Co NC

351 CAPEHART To RHODES   I Edward PIERCE a minister hereby certify that I solemnized the rites of matrimony between Wm E CAPEHART and Susan M RHODES on the 22 day of September 1868 signed Edward PIERCE

352 KNOWLES To BLOUNT   I Edward a (sic) minister hereby certify that I solemnized the rites of matrimony between John E KNOWLES and Clara J BLOUNT on the 16th day of December 1868 signed Edward PIERCE

(40) 174 State of North Carolina Bertie County
353 WILLIFORD To BOWEN   I Edward PIERCE a minister hereby certify that I solemnized the rites of matrimony between Joseph W WILLIFORD and Sallie M BOWEN on the 16th day of December 1868 signed Edward PIERCE

354 BOWEN To HENRY   I Edward PIERCE hereby certify that I solemnized the rites of Matrimony between Marcus H BOWEN and Henrietta M HENRY on the 4th day of March AD 1869 signed Edward PIERCE

355 SHAW To MORRISS   I Edward PIERCE a minister hereby certify that I Solemnized the rites of matrimony between George W SHAW And Emaline C MORRISS on the 7th day of January 1869 signed Edward PIERCE

356 JOYNER To WILLIAMS   I Benjamin (sic) hereby certify that I solemnized the rites of matrimony between JOYNER (sic) col and Penny WILLIAMS col on the 10th day of January 1869 signed Benjamin [End of entry.]

357 HARRISS To BELL   I Benjaman CLARK do hereby certify that I solemnized the rites of matrimony between Richard HARRISS And Lizzie BELL on the 20th day of December 1869 signed Benjaman CLARK

358 HYMAN To WATSON   I Benjamon CLARK do hereby certify that I solemnized the rites of matrimony between Harry HYMAN And Rosetta WATSON on the 26th day of December 1868 signed Benjamon CLARK

359 NORFLEET To DEVEREAUX   I George BISHOP hereby certify that I solemnized the rites of Matrimony between Richmond NORFLEET and Chana DEVEREAUX col on the 16th day of June A D 1870 signed George BISHOP

(41) 175 State of North Carolina Bertie County
360 MARTIN To CREASY   I Thadeous WILSON hereby certify that I solemnized the rites of matrimony between James MARTIN col and Olley CREASEY on the day of (sic) August A D 1870 signed Thadeous WILSON

361 ARMISTEAD To ALLEN   I Thadeous WILSON do hereby certify that I solemnized the rites of matrimony between Jerry ARMISTEAD col and Precilla ALLEN col on the 13th day of Aug AD 1870 signed Thadeous WILSON

362 JOHNSON To THOMPSON   I George BISHOP hereby certify that I solemnized the rites of matrimony between Turner JOHNSON and Silvia THOMPSON col on the 10th day of August AD 1870 signed George BISHOP JP

363 BROWN To MILLER   I B B WILLIAMS hereby certify that I solemnized the rites of matrimony between Thos W BROWN and Cyntha E MILLER on the 21st day of August A D 1870 signed B B WILLIAMS

364 MITCHELL To PERRY   I John MITCHELL hereby certify that I solemnized the rites of matrimony between J W MITCHELL and Laura E PERRY on the 8th day of september AD 1870 signed John MITCHELL

365 EVANS To JERNIGAN   I Moses L MIZELL minister of the Gospel hereby Certify that I solemnized the rites of matri-

1870

365 (Cont.) mony Between Thomas P EVANS and Elizabeth JERNIGAN on the third day of July AD 1870   (signed) Moses L MIZELL

366 POOL To MEBANE   I Abram MEBANE hereby Certify that I solemnized the rites of Matrimony between Ben POOL col and Winney MEBANE col on the 25th day of July A D 1870 (signed) Abram MEBANE

(42) 176 State of North Carolina Bertie County
367 NORFLEET To NORFLEET I George BISHOP hereby certify that I solemnized the rites of Matrimony between Anthony NORFLEET and Harriet NORFLEET col on the 30th day of July 1870 signed George BISHOP (JP

368 TILLARY To COWAND   I Peter MOUNTAIN J P hereby certify that I solemnized the rites of Matrimony between William TILLARY col and Harriet COWAND on the 4th day of August AD 1870 signed Peter MOUNTAIN J P

END OF BOOK

Vol.: Not numbered   Years: 1870-1872   Pages: 1-11

[Note: First page of this volume begins on following page.]

(43) 1 From 1st. Sept. 1870 Marriage Register.

#	Name of Male.	Name of Female.	Name of Father of Male.	Name of Mother of Male.	Name of Father of Female.	Name of Mother of Female.	Place of Marriage.	When Married.		2 (sic) By Whom Married
1	Isaac SMALL	Leah THOMPSON	Donaldson SMALL	Penelope SMALL	Jacob TEENCE	Margarett TEENCE	Windsor Twp.	8th. Sept.	1870	G W DOWNING J.P.
2	John BAKER	Mary C HARRELL	Timothy BAKER	Kizzie BAKER	Noah HARRELL	Mary HARRELL	Colerain "	8th. Sept.	1870	B. B. WILLIAMS B.M.
3	Henry DUNDALOW	Nancy Jane WHITE	John DUNDALOW	Eliza E? DUNDERLOW (sic)	John DUNDERLOW	Sallie WHITE	Windsor "	14" "	1870	Moses L MIZELL B.M.
4	Nero BROWN	Levinia FREEMAN	Anthony BROWN	Harriet BROWN	George FREEMAN	Violet FREEMAN	Roxobel "	24 "	1870	George BISHOP J.P.
5	Samuel HOLLOMON	Levinia POWELL	Isom HOLLOMON	Sally JENKINS	Aaron POWELL	Phebe POWELL	Woodvill "	8th. Oct.	1870	Watson LEWIS J.P.
6	Alfred WHITE	Jane MELTON	Harry WATSON	Hasty WHITE	Weston MELTON	Jane COBB	Windsor "	28th. Sept.	1870	Peter MOUNTAIN J.P.
7	Daniel STEPHENSON	Emily WATSON	Daniel STEPHENSON	Cherry STEPHENSON	Nurow WATSON	Jane WATSON	Windsor "	10th. "	1870	John G MITCHELL J.P.
8	Lewis BAZEMORE	Emeline BAZEMORE	Washington BAZEMORE	Aggy BAZEMORE	Bob LEE	Patsy LEE	" "	29th "	1870	Bryant LEE B.M.
9	Joseph W JENKINS	Martha J HALE	James O. JENKINS	Jarsay JENKINS	Joseph HALE	Unknown ===	Mitchells "	14th Aug.	1870	Joseph HOLLOMON J.P.
10	Solomon MILLER	Elizabeth AMBERS	Solomon MILLER	Mary MILLER	Henry AMBERS	(blank) AMBERS	Colerain "	30th Sep.	1870	B B WILLIAMS B.M.
11	James LEE	Delia LEE	Jessee LEE	Sarah LEE	unknown	unknown	Snakebite "	22d Oct.	1870	Bryant LEE B.M.
12	Abbert WALKER	Alice ASKEW	Oscar WALKER	Lucky HECKSTALL	"	Rose ASKEW	Windsor "	6th. Nov.	1870	Edward WOOTTEN E.M.
13	Joseph J. THOMAS	Mary D. SIMMONS	Everett THOMAS	Elizabeth THOMAS	John L BURDEN	Caroline BURDEN	Snakebite "	20th. Oct.	1870	Jeremiah BUNCH B.M.
14	Simon RUFFIN	Handy SMITH	Davy RUFFIN	Hasty RUFFIN	Jo SMITH	Sally SMITH	Woodvill "	22d Oct	1870	Bryant LEE B.M.
15	James DICKSON	Martha COOPER	David DICKSON	Eldern DICKSON	Ganvill RYON	Eliza COOPER	Windsor "	19th. Nov.	1870	Geo. W. DOWNING J.P.
16	Dick GRIFFIN	Adaline COSLY	Jim GRIFFIN	Mary GRIFFIN	Jo ROBINSON	Fanny ROBINSON	===Roxobel "	20 Sept.	1870	George BROWN J.P.
17	Jessee SHERROD	Hannah WILLIAMS	Washington SHERROD	Martha SHERROD	Drew WILLIAMS	Katy WILLIAMS	Woodville "	13 Oct.	1870	George BROWN J.P.
18	Thomas CLARK	Peggy RASCOE	Thomas HARRELL	Martha CLARK	Jack RASCOE	Hetty RASCOE	" "	6th. Nov.	1870	George BROWN J.P.
19	Thomas Payton EVANS	Elizabeth JERNIGAN	James EVANS	Mary EVANS	William JERNIGAN	Drucilla JERNIGAN	Colerain "	3d. July	1870	Moses L MIZELL B.M.
20	Ben POOL Cold	Winney MEBANE Cold	Toney MEBANE	Cherry MEBANE	unknown	unknown	Merry Hill"	25th. July	1870	Abram MEBANE B.M.
21	Anthony NORFLEET Cold	Mariah TAYLOR Cold	Anthony NORFLEET	Harriet NORFLEET	"	"	Roxobel "	30th. July	1870	George BISHOP J.P.
22	William TILLERRY Cold	Harriet COMAND Cold	Unknown	Unknown	Daniel STEPHENSON	Cherry STEPHENSON	Windsor "	4th Aug	1870	Peter MOUNTAIN "
23	Albert WAD?KINS	Mahala WILLIAMS	"	"	Unknown	Unknown	(blank) "	9 Oct.	1870	Benjn. CLARK Rev.
24	Drew WHITE	Henrietta COFFIELD	Tom WHITE	Harriet WHITE	Jacob COFFIELD	Harriet COFFIELD	Colerain "	12th Nov.	1870	John SESSOMS J.P.
25	Henry PHELPS	Cinaha BROWN	unknown	Unknown	Unknown	Unknown	" "	17th. "	1870	B B WILLIAMS B.M.
26	Rollen JORDEN	Delia WARD	Charles JORDAN	Judy FOLK	Isaac WARD	Amanda SPELLER	Windsor "	17th. "	1870	John G MITCHELL J.P.
27	Aaron THOMPSON	Jane MOORE	Gain SPELLER	Duran SPELLER	Jerry MOORE	Harriet MOORE	" "	30th "	1870	George BROWN J.P.
28	Joseph W. WHITE	Katie E. FLOYD	Harvey J. WHITE	Martha A. WHITE	Samuel FLOYD	Mary FLOYD	Roxobel "	8th Decr.	1870	Jeremiah BUNCH B.M.
29	George BOND	Celia RYON	Solomon CARTER	Unknown	Dave RYON	Mary A RYON	Windsor "	17th "	1870	Abram MEBANE
30	Willie J DUNNING	Roxanah RICE	Wiley DUNNING	Emma DUNNING	John RICE	Sarah M RICE	Mitchells "	15th. "	1870	John MITCHELL

1870

(44) 2 December & January 1870 & '71

	Name of Male.	Name of Female.	Name of Father of Male.	Name of Mother of Male.	Name of Father of Female.	Name of Mother of Female.	Place of Marriage.	When Married.	By Whom Married
31	William D PARKER	R. A. PHELPS	Henry PARKER	Frusy PARKER	Jackson PHELPS	Milly PHELPS	Roxabel Twp.	12th. Jan 1871	George BISHOP J.P.
32	Frank RAYFORD	Bettie SMITH	Johnson RAYFORD	Emma RAYFORD	James SMITH	Nancy SMITH	"	12th. " 1871	" " "
33	Isaac HECKSTALL	Mary BOND	Harry HECKSTALL	Chaney HECKSTALL	Alfred RHODES	Jane BOND	Windsor "	12th. " 1871	Peter MOUNTAIN "
34	Wm. T. PERRY	Elizabeth HUGHS	Martin PERRY	Levina PERRY	Wm. PERRY	Unknown	Whites "	12th. " 1871	George W. COBB "
35	John H. JERNIGAN	Celia W. GARDNER	William JERNIGAN	Elizabeth JERNIGAN	Wm. DRAKE	Cherity GARDNER	Snakebite "	10th. " 1871	Jeremiah BUNCH B.Minr
36	Isaac BOND	Mary Elizabeth BOND	Samuel PUGH	Rebecca PUGH	Unknown	Dicy CARTER	Windsor "	15th. " 1871	Abram MEBANE "
37	William F LEARY	Alexena DONALSON	Miles LEARY	Mary Ann LEARY	William DONALDSON	Peniny DONALDSON	Indian Woods White's "	8th. " 1871	Geo. W DOWNING J.P.
38	William H BROWN	Martha E LEE	Isaac BROWN	Nancy BROWN	David LEE	Nancy LEE	Colerain "	3d. " 1871	B. B. WILLIAMS B.Minr
39	A. C. TODD	Belinda TAYLOE	John TODD	Levina TODD	Richard R TAYLOE	Mary TAYLOE	Snakebite "	5th. " 1871	John MITCHELL "
40	Silas MITCHELL	Louisa BUNCH	Bryant MITCHELL	Ann Mariah MITCHELL	Theophilus BUNCH	Moring BUNCH	"	5th. " 1871	Bryant LEE "
41	Primas OUTLAW	Foriby CHERRY	Turner OUTLAW	Marina OUTLAW	Hill CHERRY	Zina CHERRY	Windsor "	5th. " 1871	" " "
42	Alfred PRUDEN	Betsy GILLAM	Edward PRUDEN	Hannah RICE	Martin LANSTON	Julia WHITE	"	6th. " 1871	Peter MOUNTAIN J.P.
43	York RICE	Rachel TAYLOE	Unknown	Harriet RICE	Blount TAYLOE	Peggy TAYLOE	"	29th.Decr.1870	A M CRAIG B.Minister
44	Washington CARTER	Clara BIGGS	Thomas CARTER	Jana CARTER	Unknown	Winnie BIGGS	"	31 " 1870	Bryant LEE "
45	H. W. ASKEW	A. E. GREGORY	Cullen ASKEW	Lydia ASKEW	David GREGORY	Sarah GREGORY	Merry Hill"	28th. " 1870	Geo. W. COBB J.P.
46	Jo CHERRY	Mary OUTLAW	Ben CHERRY	Emeline CHERRY	Turner OUTLAW	Marina OUTLAW	Windsor "	29th. " 1870	Bryant LEE B.Minister
47	Joseph J. WHITE	Missouri BEASLEY	Luke WHITE	Penelope WHITE	J. W. BEASLEY	Julia A. BEASLEY	Colerain "	29th. " 1870	John W SESSONS J.P.
48	Willie WILLIAMS	Rose THOMAS	Unknown	Unknown	Bob THOMAS	Sophia CAPEHART	Merry Hill"	27th. " 1870	Thadeus WILSON B.Min.
49	Bill FREEMAN	Aniky WILLIAMS	Bill HOGGARD	Jane HOGGARD	Bill DEMPSY	Penny WILLIAMS	"	27th. " 1870	" " "
50	Alfred MC.GLAUHON	Malvina HOLLEY	George MC GLAUHON	Susan MC GLAUHON	Ben BROWN	Susan BROWN	Whites "	7th. Jan.1871	Geo. W COBB J.P.
51	Carson FULCHER	Emiline PERRY	Unknown	Unknown	Wilson OUTLAW	Unknown	Colerain "	28th.Decr.1870	John W SESSONS "
52	Starky HENDRIX	Jane CHERRY	Anthony HENDRIX	Mariah HENDRIX	George WESTON	Ann WESTON	Snakebite "	25th. " 1870	Bryant LEE B.Minister
53	Ceasor HECKSTALL	Amy CAPEHART	Jerry ALLEN	Hannah HECKSTALL	Unknown	Unknown	Merry Hill"	24th. " 1870	Thadeus WILSON "
54	King L CLARK	Amy RUFFIN	Hoodus CLARK	Lara CLARK	Bynum RUFFIN	Silvia RUFFIN	Woodvill"	25th. " 1870	George BROWN J.P.
55	George WATSON	Betsy RUFFIN	Dick WATSON	Rose WATSON	Adam RUFFIN	Mary RUFFIN	"	25th. " 1870	" " "
56	Stephen RUFFIN	Silva WATSON	Ephraim RUFFIN	Easter RUFFIN	John WATSON	Jane BOND	"	25th. " 1870	" " "
57	Cubit CLARK	Harriet E RUFFIN	Ben CLARK	Louisa CLARK	Patterson RUFFIN	Patint RUFFIN	"	26th. " 1870	" " "
58	Freeman CLARK	Edy VICK	Unknown	Sarah CLARK	Croford POWELL	Martha POWELL	"	24th. " 1870	" " "
59	Jessee CLARK	Liddy PUGH	Jubiter CLARK	Violet CLARK	Liss? CLARK	Phillis PUGH	Roxobel "	29th. " 1870	Benj CLARK B.Min
60	Isaac ASKEW	Perlina WARD	Isaac ASKEW	Jenney ASKEW	Ned WYNNS	Nancy WYNNS	Mitchells"	22d. " 1870	John MITCHELL B.Min.

(45) 3 December & January 1870 & '71 Marriage Register.

#	Name of Male.	Name of Female.	Name of Father of Male.	Name of Mother of Male.	Name of Father of Female.	Name of Mother of Female.	Place of Marriage.	When Married	By Whom Married
61	Harry OUTLAW	Mary E. OUTLAW	Henry OUTLAW	Margaet OUTLAW	Alfred OUTLAW	Lucy OUTLAW	Merry Hill Twp.	25th.Decr.1870	Thadeus WILSON B.Min.
62	Ned WHITUS	Jennett POWELL	Peter WHITUS	Caty WHITUS	Jim POWELL	Martha POWELL	Windsor	19th. " 1870	John G MITCHELL J.P.
63	Charles WATSON	Judy RYON	Unknown	Unknown	Unknown	Hanna BOND	"	24th. " 1870	Bryant LEE B.Minister
64	Peter HAYS	Belinda MORRISS	Jacob ALEMOND	Fanny HAYS	Noah CHERRY	Jane MORRISS	"	17th. " 1870	A M CRAIG B.Minister
65	Stephen ADKISSON	Mary BOND	Major WOOLERD	Molly ADKISON	Anthony BOND	Mahala BELL	"	2d Jan. 1871	Peter MOUNTAIN J.P.
66	William T. SHAW	William A TODD(sic)	John SHAW	Frances SHAW	Alfred EASON	Mary FLOOD	"	15th Decr.1870	David HARRELL B.Min.
67	Jacob JOHNSON	Ann TEAMER	Ben JOHNSON	Rachel JOHNSON	Jack TEAMER	Emeline TEAMER	"	13th. " 1870	Geo. W DOWNING J.P.
68	Thomas VALENTINE	Adaline WATFORD	Isaac VALENTINE	Betty VALENTINE	Droy WATFORD	Unknown	Colerain	26th.Nov. 1870	Emanuel RAYNOLDS
69	Jacob HOLLAND	Elizabeth TAYLOE	Henry HOLLAND	Harriet HOLLAND	Emanuel PETERSON	Matilda PETERSON	Snakebite	7th. Jan.1871	Bryant LEE B.Minister
70	Charles HOLLEY	Hester PELT	William BROWN	Harriet BROWN	Cooper PELT	Mariah PELT	Colerain	7th. " 1871	Emanuel RAYNOLDS
71	Joseph WATSON	Caroline BAZEMORE	Dempsey MILLER	Mariah WATSON	Fred BAZEMORE	(blank)	Snakebite	10th. " 1871	Bryant LEE B.Minister
72	Madison BACKUS	Mariah WEBSTER	Thomas BACKUS	Sarah BACKUS	(blank)	Debora ETHERIDGE	Colerain	14th. " 1871	John W SESSOMS J.P.
73	George CHERRY	Muriah BURDEN	Noah CHERRY Sr.	Levina CHERRY	Lewis BURDEN	Gracy BURDEN	Snakebite	15th. " 1871	Bryant LEE Bap.Minis
74	Robert SPIVEY	Kezziah SPIVEY	George SPIVEY	Cinthy SPIVEY	Noah CHERRY	Mariah CHERRY	"	19th. " 1871	"
75	Gustavus P HALL	Elizabeth S NICHOLLS	John H. HALL	Margaret Y HALL	Thomas B NICHOLLS	Martha NICHOLLS	Windsor	25th. " 1871	Edwd. WOOTTEN Episc. Minist
76	Lewis SPIVEY	Arabella JONES	Henry LEVEN	Caroline SPIVEY	Britton JONES	Isabella JONES	"	26th. " 1871	Peter MOUNTAIN J.P.
77	A. J. COFFIELD	Emily C SHAW	John COFFIELD	Elizabeth COFFIELD	James SHAW	Neonia SHAW	Merry Hill	29th. " 1871	James H SMITH
78	Thomas H PARKER	R E PRITCHARD	John PARKER	Emeline PARKER	Outlaw PRITCHARD	Mrs (blank) HINES	Woodville==	2d Feb. 1871	Jeremiah BUNCH B.Min.
79	Allen GILLAM	Jane OUTLAW	Guye GILLAM	Rachel GILLAM	James OUTLAW	Rachel OUTLAW	Merry Hill	3d. Jan. 1871	Thadeus WILSON "
80	Daniel ROBBINS	Penelope OUTLAW	Bob ROBBINS	Hannah ROBBINS	Alfred OUTLAW	Lucy OUTLAW	"	8th. " 1871	" "
81	George E. EVANS	Martha R. PHELPS	Edwin EVINS	Mary EVANS	Micajah PHELPS	Ann Rebecca PHELPS	"	12th.Feb 1871	George W COBB J.P.
82	Blount RAYNER	Annis WHITE	Cyntha RAYNER	Cyntha RAYNER	Lewis WHITE	Hannah WHITE	Colerain	12th. " 1871	G. N. GREEN
83	Moses HOGGARD	Zilphy MEBANE	Ben OUTLAW	Nancy HOGGARD	Andy MEBANE	Sabra MEBANE	Windsor	13th. " 1871	David HARRELL B.Minis
84	Peter CARTER	Lucy WILLIAMS	Solomon NICHOLLS	Emma CARTER	Alfred WILSON	Janice COTTON	"	18th. " 1871	Peter MOUNTAIN J.P.
85	Mirabana L WOOD	Margaret A. COTTON	Richard WOOD	Mrs Mary WOOD	Lewis COTTON	Pattie C. COTTON	Roxobel	22d. Feb. 1871	Edwd. WOOTTEN Episc. Minist
86	William LEGGETT	Fannie MIZELL	Nebuchadnezer LEGGETT	Penicy LEGGETT	James MIZELL	Syntha MIZELL	Windsor	23d " 1871	David HARRELL B. Minist
87	Peter LEE	Lucy PEELE	Isam SHARROCK	Delia LEE	Ned PEELE	Rose PEELE	Roxobel	5th.Jan. 1871	George BISHOP J.P.
88	London HYMAN	Mary C WILLIAMS	Abram DOSSEY	Rebecca DOSSEY	Freeman WILLIAMS	(blank)	Woodville	15th. " 1871	" BROWN "
89	Richard COX	Martha DAVIS	Essex PEELE	Violet PEELE	James LAUGHFORD	Rebecca DAVIS	(blank)	27th. " 1871	" BISHOP "
90	John HUGHS	Mary Eliza WILLFORD	(blank)	(blank)	John WILLFORD	Absaly WILLFORD	(blank)	2d Mar. 1871	Jeremiah BUNCH B. Minist

1870/1871

(46) 4 Marriage Register.

	Name of Male.	Name of Female.	Name of Father of Male.	Name of Mother of Male.	Name of Father of Female.	Name of Mother of Female.	Place of Marriage.	When Married		By Whom Married
91	George HILL	Silva BOND	Frank CORBIT	Vilet BIDDLE	Arch PUGH	Cloa BOND	Windsor Twp.	4th.	Mar.1871	Geo W DOWNING J.P.
92	Joseph THOMPSON	Olive PEELE	Parents unknown		Parents unknown		Snakebite	2d.	" 1871	Bryant LEE Bap.Min.
93	George W = HOBBS	Elenor FREEMAN	Joseph HOBBS	Mary HOBBS	George W LANE	Katie LANE	Colerain	12th.	Jan.1871	B.B.WILLIAMS Bap.Min.
94	Guye PUGH	Polly RUFFIN	Solomon PUGH	Aggy PUGH	Aaron SHARROCK	Winnie RUFFIN	Woodvile	24th.	" 1871	George BROWN J.P.
95	John D. CASTELLOW	Winnie Ann HARRISON	Larry CASTELLOW	Vallie CASTELLOW	George HARRIS(sic)	Penelope HARRISSON	Windsor	19th.	" 1871	Moses L MIZELL Bap. Miy?
96	Thomas SMITH	Antonetta DUNNING	unknown	do	do	do	Roxobel	10th.	" 1871	Richard E L COX J.P.
97	Alfred MITCHELL	Cherry DUNNING					"	14th.	" 1871	B. B. WILLIAMS Bap.Min.
98	Gaston H. NORRISS	Fannie E. WHITE	James L NORRISS	Kerron NORRISS	Josiah WHITE	Martha WHITE	Colerain	9th.	Feb.1871	"
99	Joseph D EVANS	Sallie A PERRY	Starky R EVANS	Mary EVANS	George W PERRY	Martha A PERRY	"	16th.	" 1871	Moses L MIZELL " "
100	Wm. T WHITE	Kiddy WHITE	William WHITE	Ludy WHITE	Kader WHITE	Harriet WHITE	"	22d.	" 1871	" " " "
101	Isom THOMPSON	Penelopy EPPS	Henry EPPS	Penelopy EPPS	Freeman WILLIAMS	Penelope WILLIAMS	Woodville	22d.	" 1871	George BROWN J.P.
102	Darius R MITCHELL	Nancy C. MILLER	King MITCHELL	Rebecca MITCHELL	David MILLER	Sarah MILLER	Colerain	30th.	" 1871	B B WILLIAMS Bap.Min.
103	Henry JENKINS	Mary Ann BOON	Nat JENKINS	Clarisy GRIFFIN	Tom BOON	Rindy BOON	"	4th.	Mar.1871	John W SESSOMS J.P.
104	James JOHNSON	Julia GORDEN	A JOHNSON	Rachel JOHNSON	Edward GORDEN	Nancy GORDEN	"	14th.	" 1871	"
105	George A. COOPER	Sarah OUTLAW	Isaac WARD	Amanda SPELLER	George OUTLAW	Rachel WARD	Windsor	25th.	" 1871	Henry D COOPER "
106	Ezekiel DANIEL	Mary E. JERNIGAN	Eli DANIEL	Fannie DANIEL	William JERNIGAN	unknown	Colerain	8th.	" 1871	Moses L MIZELLBap.Min.
107	James H HARRELL	Nancy E. PARKER	James HARRELL	Lisha HARRELL	Samuel PARKER	Elizabeth PARKER	Roxobel	9th.	" 1871	Richd. E L COX J.P.
108	Ceasor GILLAM	Sarah CLARK	Ceasor GILLAM	Matilda GILLAM	Jerry CLARK	Lovey CLARK	Windsor	14th.	" 1871	Peter MOUNTAIN "
109	J. W. MILES	Mary E. HARDY	Benjn. MILES	Charlotte MILES	Thos. B HARDY	Carrie HARDY	Woodvill	8th.	" 1871	J W COMPTON Methdst. Minist
110	John HOGGARD	Mary W JENKINS	David HOGGARD	Rebecca HOGGARD	George JENKINS	Mary JENKINS	Roxobel	23d.	" 1871	Jeremiah BUNCHBap.Min.
111	Eli ASKEW	Willie A WARD	Unknown	Rosetia ASKEW	Dembry WARD	Sarah E WARD	Windsor	30th.	" 1871	"
112	Shadrick WATSON	Muriah WATSON	Ben DISON	Charity BRITTON	Arter GILLAM	Rachel WATSON	Windsor	17th.	Jan 1871	AM CRAIG Bap. Minist
113	James ROBINSON	Mariah CLARK	George ROBINSON	Unknown	Emanuel CLARK	Unknown	Roxobe	12th.	Mar 1871	Benj. CLARK Minister of Gos
114	Wm. A. SANDERLIN	Leueza TREADWELL	Majah BERN	Eley BERN	Unknown	Sarah TREADWELL	Merry Hill	16th.	" 1871	Thadeus WILSONBap.Min
115	John ALLEN	Jane ROBBINS	Jack ALLEN	Rachel ALLEN	Bob ROBBINS	Hannah ROBBINS	"	17th.	" 1871	"
116	John CLARK	Mariah A. HENTON	Hampton THOMPSON	Diner THOMPSON	Nathan (blank)	Annie URQUHART	Woodville	23d	" 1871	George BROWN J.P.
117	Nathan THOMPSON	Elcy BALLANCE	David JOHNSON	Rachel PUGH	Moses DEBREAUX	Mima WILLIAMS	"	23d	" 1871	"
118	Henry WILKINS	Manny WILLIAMS	Parents unknown		(blank)	(blank)	"	23d	" 1871	Benjn. CLARK Minis Gos
119	William PUGH	Jane RUFFIN	Will PUGH	Celia PUGH	Ephraim RUFFIN	Easter RUFFIN	"	26th.	" 1871	George BROWN J.P.
120	Joseph JOHNSON	Fabra BAZEMORE	Jack JOHNSON	Eliza JOHNSON	Reddick HOLDER	Hannah BAZEMORE	Mitchell's	2d	April 1871	John MITCHELL Bap.Min

1871

(47) 5 Marriage Register.

Name of Male.	Name of Female.	Name of Father of Male.	Name of Mother of Male.	Name of Father of Female.	Name of Mother of Female.	Place of Marriage.	When Married	By Whom Married
121-Primos RASCOE	Annis BOND	Granville RASCOE	Hetty RASCOE	Brister BOND	Cloe BOND	Windsor Twp.	8th April 1871	Geo. W DOWING J.P.
122-Abram WILLIAMS	Aggy TYLER	Thos. WILLIAMS	not known	George TYLER	Sallie TYLER	Woodville "	23d. " 1871	Geo. BROWN J.P.
123-Ebenezer PRICE	Mary JENKINS	John PRICE	Sally PRICE	Joseph JENKINS	Patsy JENKINS	Mitchells "	13th. " 1871	Jerremiah BUNCH Bap.Min
124-William TAYLOR	Sarah NORFLEET	Richard EVRITT	Hannah TORVELL?	Byrum MINTON	Sarah MINTON	Roxobel "	15th. " 1871	Bryant LEE Bap.Minister
125-George JERNIGAN	Sarah MORRISS	Alfred JERNIGAN	Sally JERNIGAN	Allen MORRISS	Sally MORRISS	Woodville "	4th.May 1871	Watson LEWIS J.P.
126-Daniel W. WHITE	Mary RAYNER	Lewis WHITE	Vilet1 WHITE	Unknown	Sintha RAYNER	Colerain "	7 " 1871	G. M. GREEN J.P.
127-Augustus DEMPSY	Penny JOHNSON	Whitmelle DEMPSY	Elizabeth DEMPSEY	Jack JOHNSON	Elizabeth JOHNSON	Merry Hill "	11 " 1871	J W SMITH J.P.
128-James JONES	Martha FANNING	Simon FREEMAN	Minney JONES	Alfred PUGH	Silva FANNING	Windsor "	14th. " 1871	Bryant LEE Bap.Min
129-Frank SINGLETON	Cherry WEBB	Roscoe SINGLETON	Rebecca SINGLETON	Logan WEBB	Lucinda WEBB	" "	14th. " 1871	" " "
130-Edward PEARCE	Sallie KEETER	William PEARCE	Mary PEARCE	John KEETER	Sallie KEETER	Merry Hill "	22d " 1871	James W SMITH JP.
131-John L GRIFFIN	Mary L. SMALLWOOD	John B. GRIFFIN	Sarah E? GRIFFIN	Charles SMALLWOOD	Harriet SMALLWOOD	Woodville "	27th April 1871	Edwd. WOOTEN Epis.Min.
132-Edward BARNHILL	Virginia ROSS	Wash BARNHILL	Tincy? BARNHILL	Isaac ROSS	Perneny ROSS	Windsor "	4th.May 1871	John G MITCHELL J.P.
133-William GORDEN	Jane MORGAN	Ned BACCUS cold	Unknown	Unknown	Unknown	Colerain "	20th. " 1871	J. W. SESSOMS J.P.
134-George BOOKER	Aggy COOPER Cold	Unknown	"	Dick WATSON	Tempy WATSON	Windsor "	27th. " 1871	H. C. COOPER Cold J.P.
135-Burges URQUHART	Mary B. THOMPSON	Dr Richard A. URQUHART	Mary R URQUHART	Lewis THOMPSON	Margaret A. THOMPSON	Woodvill "	6th.June 1871	Edwd. WOOTEN Epis.Minr.
136-Wm. G COGGAN	Frances E WYNNS	Wm. G. COGGAN	Winiford COGGAN	Robert WILLFORD	Elizabeth WILLFORD	Windsor "	24th.May 1871	Jerremiah BUNCH BapMin
137-Frederic BUNCH	Martha GREEN	Cullen BUNCH	Rhoda BUNCH	== Noah E GREEN	Susan GREEN	Colerain "	8th.June 1871	John W. SESSOMS J.P.
138-T. A. BURROWO	Mary A. PITMAN	John BURROW	Frances LENIER	Z PITMAN	Unknown	Windsor "	15th. " 1871	J. W. COMPTON MethMin
139-Hardy RASCOE	Sarah EICHE	Granvil RASCOE	Hetty RASCOE	James EICHE	Hetty RASCOE (sic)	" "	17th. " 1871	J. G. MITCHELL J.P.
140-Yancy EVANS	Martha MIZELL	James EVANS	Mary EVANS	Josiah MIZELL	Nancy MIZELL	" "	18th.May 1871	Moses MIZELL Bap.Minis
141-William WEBB	Emily WHITE	Logan WEBB	Lucindy WEBB	David WHITE	Marina WHITE	" "	10th.June 1871	Bryant LEE Bap.Minis
142-Wm. HARGRAVE	Hannah PUGH Cold	Unknown	Nancy HARGRAVE	Ben OUTLAW	Adaline PUGH	Snakebite "	18th. " 1871	" " "
143-David SPELLER	Jane SPELLER Cold	George SPELLER	Eady SPELLER	Oscar SPELLER	Patience SPELLER	Windsor "	18th. " 1871	Abram MEBANE Bap.Min
144-John BLOUNT	Jane ROULHAC Cold	Gusther BLOUNT	Katie BLOUNT	Hanibel JOHNSON	Rebecca JOHNSON	" "	19th. " 1871	John G MITCHELL (J.P.)
145-Willis THOMPSON	Emma BROWN Cold	Amos THOMPSON	Winnie THOMPSON	unknown	unknown	Woodville "	13th. " 1869	G. M. MITCHELL (J.P.)
146-John H. THOMAS	Eveline SWAIN Cold	Tom RHODES	Patient WEST	Ned MORISS	Tempy MILLER	Windsor "	13th. " 1871	John G MITCHELL.J.P.
147-R. W. COFFIELD	Celia A. PERRY	Alfred COFFIELD	Deliah COFFIELD	Dossey PERRY	Rachel PERRY	Colerain "	11th.May 1871	Geo. W COBB J.P.
148-James W. LANGLEY	Ann BARNACASCLE	James LANGLEY	Ann LANGLEY	Geo. W BARNACASCLE	Susan BARNACASCLE	Merry Hill "	22d June 1871	J W SMITH J.P.
149-Charles HASON	Silva WILLIAMS	Speaker HASON	Milly HASON	Solomon WILLIAMS	Mary WILLIAMS	Windsor "	27th. " 1871	John G MITCHELL J.P.
150-Blount THOMAS	Adaline POWELL	Daniel MITCHELL	Rhoda JENKINS	Wm. POWELL	Adaline POWELL	" "	1 July 1871	Peter MOUNTAIN J.P. gone to Liberia} Nov. 1871. }

(48) 6 Marriage Register.

Name of Male.	Name of Female.	Name of Father of Male.	Name of Mother of Male.	Name of Father of Female.	Name of Mother of Female.	Place of Marriage.	When Married.		By Whom Married
151-Calvin J. MORRISS	Fannie M. NEWSOM	James L MORRISS	Carol MORRISS	Joseph NEWSOM	unknown	Colerain Twp.	4th. July	1871	B. B. WILLIAMS Bap.Min
152-Jos. P. PEARCE	Martha E. PERRY	Hardy PEARCE	Hester PEARCE	Martin PERRY	Lavena PERRY	White's	6th.	1871	Geo. W COBB J.P.
153-Joseph BOSKY	Jane BUTLER	Foreigner	(blank)	unknown	unknown	Windsor	6th.	1871	J W. COMPTON M.E.Minis
154-Shadrick COBB	Marinda MEBANE	Shadrick COBB	Hester COBB	Allin MEBANE	Amelia MEBANE	White's	8th.	1871	Geo. W COBB. J.P.
155-David BOND	Malvina ETHERIDGE	Valdo BOND	Sallie BOND	Unknown	Rebecca CARTER	Windsor	8th.	1871	P. MOUNTAIN J.P.
156-Kenneth WHITE	Nancy BROWN	Medea WHITE	Martha WHITE	Benjn. BROWN	Syntha BROWN	White's	20th.	1871	S. T. HUGHES J.P.
157-Wright PEARCE	Fannie WHITE	William PEARCE	Mary BALDIN	Henry WHITE	Sophia WHITE	Windsor	27th.	1871	John G MITCHELL J.P.
158-Edward STEPHENSON	Martha BOND	William SWAIN	Mariah WARD	Bristas BOND	Mariah BOND	"	29th.	1871	" "
159-Henry TURPIN	Jane CHERRY	Unknown	Unknown	Bryant CHERRY	Hannah CHERRY	"	30th.	1871	Benjn. F KING Bap.Minis
160-George M. CASPER	Sarah E. POWELL	William CASPER	Peggy CASPER	Richard POWELL	Mary POWELL	Snakebite	3d. Aug.	1871	Jeremiah BUNCH "
161-Joseph BAZEMORE	Celia A DUNNING	John BAZEMORE	Penny BAZEMORE	Ned DUNNING	Antenett DUNNING	Roxobel	9th.	1871	R E L COX J.P.
162-Joseph RASCOE	Judy HARRELL	Fedrick BOND ====	Susan RASCOE	Hab BAZEMORE	Patience HARRELL	Windsor	10th.	1871	Bryant LEE Bap Mins
163-Armstead COOPER	William Ann COOPER	Unknown	Adaline COOPER	Unknown	Rebecca COOPER	"	13th.	1871	" "
164-Jos. W. BAZEMORE	Nancy CASPER	William BAZEMORE	Rebecca BAZEMORE	Jared CASPER	Mary CASPER	"	13th.	1871	Jeremiah BUNCH Bap.Min
165-Madison SMALLWOOD	Eliza VICK	Unknown	Liszina SMALLWOOD	Unknown	Penelope WALTON	Woodville	16th.	1871	Bryant LEE Bap.Minis
166-James S TODD	Penelope HARRELL	Hardy TODD	Sally TODD	Elisha MITCHELL	Mary MITCHELL	Snate-bite"	30th.	1871	B. F. BARBER Bap.Minis

From September 1871

	Name of Male	Name of Female	Father of Male	Mother of Male	Father of Female	Mother of Female	Place	When		By Whom
1-	John BUNCH	Elizabeth CHERRY	Alaxander BOON	Rose BUNCH	Unknown	Ann CHERRY	Snakebite	8th.Sept.	1871	Bryant LEE Bap. Min
2-	George TAYLOE	Ann FREEMAN	Lawrance TAYLOE	Eliza TAYLOE	Bryant FREEMAN	Nelly FREEMAN	Woodville	8th.	1871	Emanuel RENALDS "
3.	Robert CARTER	Zilpha BOND	King COOPER	Mary Jane WATSON	Solomon CARTER	Daffy BOND	Windsor	9th.	1871	G. W DOWNING J.P.
4.	Knowledge BARROW	Louisa WILLIAMS	David CLARK	Krissy BARROW	Unknown	Serena WILLIAMS	Woodville	10th.	1871	Benjn. CLARK Bap.Min
5.	Thompson GRAY	Marinda WILLIAMS	Plato GRAY	Cherry GRAY	Unknown	Unknown	Merry Hill"	13th.	1871	H C COOPER J.P.
6.	Clark GASKINS	Molly SPRUELL	Unknown	Unknown	"		Colerain	17th.	1871	Jno. W SESSONS J.P.
7.	John POWELL ====	Flora BOND	Solomon RUFFIN	Rhoda POWELL	Samuel PUGH	Rebecca BOND	Windsor	21st.	1871	G W DOWNING J.P.
8.	Henry WHITE	Julia TAYLOE	Harry MORRIS	Louisa WHITE	Lewis WHITE	Nancy TAYLOE	Colerain	23d	1871	G. N. GREEN J.P.
9.	Robert SMALLWOOD	Ann BOND	Jack PUGH	Sabry RUFFIN	Lewis T BOND	Cherry BOND	Windsor	30th.	1871	G W DOWNING J.P.
10.	Amariah DEMPSY	Gilla COFFIELD	Jessee DEMPSY	Unknown	Benjn. COFFIELD	Delilah COFFIELD	Merry Hill"	1st Oct.	1871	G W COBB J.P.
11.	Ephraim RUFFIN	Cottie RASCOE	Dempsy POWELL	Bettie RUFFIN	Andy HARDRE	Fairiba RASCOE	Winds(sic)"	6th.	1871	Jas. T RAYNER J.P.

1871

(49) 7 Marriage Register.

	Name of Male.	Name of Female.	Name of Father of Male.	Name of Mother of Male.	Name of Father of Female.	Name of Mother of Female.	Place of Marriage.	When Married			By Whom Married
12.	Thomas HUNT	Sarah MITCHELL	Lawson HUNT	Rachel HUNT	Drew OUTLAW	Polly OUTLAW	MerryHillTwp.	7th.	Oct.	1871	Henry C COOPER J.P.
13.	Jefferson WILLIAMS	Sylvesta URQUHART	Robert WILLIAMS	Annis WILLIAMS	Luke URQUHART	Celia URQUHART	Woodville "	21st.	"	1871	Benjn. CLARK Bap.Min.
14.	Alexander JONES	Margaret PERRY	Dossey JONES	Celia JONES	Charles HENRY	Rose PERRY	Colerain "	22d.	"	1871	J W SESSOMS J.P.
15.	Andrew SESSOMS	Emma PERRY	Andrew PERRY	Moring PERRY	Clem WARD	Esther PERRY	" "	27th.	"	1871	B.B WILLIAMS Bap.Min
16.	Sandy MOORE	Mary LAW	Moses MOORE	Sarah MOORE	Pennie LAW (sic)	Peter LAW (sic)	Merry Hill"	27th.	"	1871	Thaddeus WILSON " "
17.	Lewis DOUGLAS	Rachel MOORE	George DOUGLAS	Bettie DOUGLAS	George MOORE	Sallie MOORE	" "	27th.	"	1871	" " " "
18.	Solomon RHODES	Alice RHODES	Thomas RHODES	Phillis RHODES	Isaac CAPEHART	Adaline CAPEHART	" "	27th.	"	1871	" " " "
19.	Outlaw PUGH	Phebe RASCOE	Ben OUTLAW	Rachel OUTLAW	Bob OUTLAW	Annis RASCOE	Windsor "	28th.	"	1871	Wm. WALTON J.P.
20.	William TASWELL	Ann PUGH	Edward TASWELL	Eliza TASWELL	James CRAIG	Rosetta CRAIG	Woodville "	28th.	"	1871	" " "
21.	Bryant PERRY	Venus MORING	Thos. WHITE	Violet PERRY?	Unknown	Unknown	Colerain "	2d	Nov.	1871	G N. GREEN "
22.	Hill J. CASTELLOW	Narcissa WHITE	Levi CASTELLOW	Patsy CASTELLOW	Wright WHITE	Katy WHITE	Windsor "	2d.	"	1871	David HARRELL Bap.Min.
23.	Isaiah DONALDSON	Penelope Ann JOHNSON	William DONALDSON	Peniah DONALDSON	Enoch JOHNSON	Winny JOHNSON	" "	7th.	"	1871	Edward PEARCE " "
24.	Dr Benjn. M. WALKER	Miss Harriet E PUGH	Jordan WALKER	Martha A WALKER	Wm. A PUGH	Harriet T. PUGH	Snakebite "	7th.	"	1871	Edwd. WOOTTEN Episl. Minist
25.	Rev. Edwd. WOOTTEN	Miss Julia W TAYLOE	Shadrick WOOTTEN	Mary E WOOTTEN	Jonathan S TAYLOE	Prudence TAYLOE	Windsor "	8th.	"	1871	Luther EBUN " "
26.	Jos. S PARKER	Mary M COX	Laml PARKER	Elizabeth PARKER	Moore RAWLS	Mary RAWLS	Snakebite "	8th.	"	1871	Jeremiah BUNCH Bap M.
27.	Henry MIZELL	Barbary WHITE	Lewis ELLYSON	Eady MIZELL	Nelson WHITE	Caroline WHITE	Colerain "	11th.	"	1871	J W SESSOMS J.P.
28.	Turner COBB	Priscilla HOLLY	Shade COBB	Hester RAYE?	David HOLLEY	Patsy HOLLEY	Whites "	11th.	"	1871	James T. RAYNER " "
29.	West MILLER	Priscilla WHITE	John MILLER	Penelope MILLER	Jonathan WADEN?	Mary MIZELL	" "	15th.	"	1871	" " " "
30.	James D BRICKLE	Harriet E MIZELL	James BRICKEL	Nancy BRICKEL	Thos. MIZELL	Delily MIZELL	Merry Hill"	28th.	"	1871	James W SMITH " "
31.	Thos SMITHWICK	Joana PHELPS	Samuel SMITHWICK	Martha A.SMITHWICK	Asa PHELPS	Elizabeth PHELPS	" "	30th.	"	1871	J. M. C. LUKE Bap.Min
32.	Jacob W TODD	Ann Sawyer WHITE	Elisha TODD	Basha TODD	William WHITE	(blank)	Windsor "	30th.	"	1871	Abner WHITE J.P.
33.	Jas.H BARNACASLE	Elizabeth PHELPS	Geo. W BARNACASLE	Susan BARNACASLE	John PHELPS	Susan PHELPS	" "	3d	Decr.	1871	Edwd.WOOTTEN Epis.Minis
34.	Trim WOOD	Isabella FAGANS	Charles TOMS	Harriet WOOD	Henry FAGANS	Amanda FAGANS	Merry Hill"	4th.	"	1871	Thaddeus WILSON Bap."
35.	Jefferson NICHOLLS	Mary CAPEHART	Moses NICHOLLS	Penelope NICHOLLS	Antony CAPEHART	Esther WILLIAMS	" "	3d	"	1871	" " " "
36.	Charles S. JENKINS	Miss Elizabeth DUNNING	George JENKINS	Mary JENKINS	Lazarus DUNNING	Harriet DUNNING	Roxobel "	7th.	"	1871	Jeremiah BUNCH " "
37.	William J CASPER	Adaline COOPER	William J CASPER	Margaret CASPER	Asa COOPER	Elizabeth COOPER	Snakebite "	7th.	"	1871	" " " "
38.	Watson MITCHELL	Celia A MEBANE	George JERNIGAN	Celia JERNIGAN	Solomon (sic)	Marina MEBANE	Whites "	7th.	"	1871	G W COBB J.P.
39.	Henry WILKINS	Louisa JONES	Harreald WINSON	Abby WILKINS	Willis JONES	Silvy JONES	Woodville "	7th.	"	1871	Benjn. CLARK Bap.Min.
40.	George JONES	Hasty MEBANE	George JONES	Barbry JONES	Nathan MEBANE	Venus MEBANE	Whites "	9th.	"	1871	Jas. T RAYNER J.P.
41.	George W HOGGARD	Celia A PERRY	Minor HOGGARD	Ludia HOGGARD	Daniel PERRY	Nancy PERRY	Colerain "	10th.	"	1871	G. N. GREEN " "

(50) 8 Marriage Register

	Name of Male.	Name of Female.	Name of Father of Male.	Name of Mother of Male.	Name of Father of Female.	Name of Mother of Female.	Place of Marriage.	When Married.		By Whom Married
42.	John W. SMITH	Sarah E BIRD	Elijah SMITH	Eliza SMITH	Willie BIRD	Sarah BIRD	Colerain Twp.	13th.	Decr.1871	B B WILLIAMS Bap. Min
43.	William D BIRD	Susan A HOLLOMON	Willie BIRD	Sarah BIRD	Whitmill HOLLOMON	Emily M HOLLOMON	"	14th.	" 1871	John W SESSOMS J.P.
44.	William SMITH	Rebecca CULLIPHER	John SMITH	Nancy SMITH	James CULLIPHER	Rebecca CULLIPHER	Merry Hill	14th.	" 1871	Edwd. PEARCE Bap.Min
45.	Cesar SMALLWOOD	Abby LEE	Ben SMALLWOOD	Priscy SMALLWOOD	Bob LEE	Patsy LEE	Woodvill	28th.	" 1871	Wm. WALTON J. P.
46.	Andrew CRAIG	Pattie GILLAM	Rev. A M CRAIG	Mary Ann CRAIG	Willie J GILLAM	E R GILLAM	Windsor	15th.	" 1871	A. M. CRAIG Bap M.
47.	James E TREVATHAN	Mary E MARRISS	John E TRAVATHAN	Pleasant TRAVATHAN	John MORRISS	Mary MARRISS	Marry Hill	17th.	" 1871	J W SMITH J. P.
48.	Jacob ROGERS	Lucy TAYLOE	Unknown	Anichy GARRETT	Ralph TYLER	Rose ASKEW	Roxobel	21st.	" 1871	John MITCHELL Bap. M.
49.	George W WHITE	Mary E BAZEMORE	Starky WHITE	Emily WHITE	Alder == BAZEMORE	Emeline BAZEMORE	Snakebite	21st.	" 1871	J. BUNCH Bap. Min
50.	Joseph D KENIDY	Nicy E MIZELL	Baldy KENIDY	Mary KENEDY	James MIZELL	Cyntha MIZELL	Windsor	21st.	" 1871	David HARRELL " "
51.	Dennison WORTHINGTON	Julia M MEBANE	Dr Robt. H WORTHINGTON	Elizabeth WORTHINGTON	Dr Saml. J WHEELER	Lucinda B WHEELER	"	23	Nov. 1871	A. M. CRAIG
52.	Augustus JERMIGAN	Ann M DONALDSON	George JERMIGAN	Penny CALE	William DONALDSON	Penina DONALDSON	"	26	Decr.1872	J W COMPTON Meth
53.	Slade ROBBINS	Adaline CLARK	Edward ROBBINS	Violet ROBBINS	Harklas CLARK	Lawra CLARK	Woodville	26	" 1871	Thos. W SKIRVIN J.P.
54.	William A CASPER	Celia E BUTLER	Thomas CASPER	Marina CASPER	James BUTLER	Jane BUTLER	Snakebite	26	" 1871	J BUNCH Bap. Min
55.	Hinton MORRISS	Martha HOGGARD	Ben MORRISS	Mary MORRISS	Minor HOGGARD	Ludia HOGGARD	Colerain	26	" 1871	G. M. GREEN J. P.
56.	Cisaro WEST	Emma NICHOLLS	Mead WEST	Ellen WEST	Bob NICHOLLS	Hester NICHOLLS	Merry Hill	27	" 1871	Thaddeus WILSON B M
57.	George P PERRY	Joanna CASTELLOW	Martin PERRY	Lavenia PERRY	Henry CASTELLOW	Caroline BIRD	Windsor	27	" 1871	J W COMPTON M. Min
58.	Frank CLARK	Laura HODGE	Turner WILLIAMS	Hasty CLARK	Freeman BELL	Minnie HODGE	Woodville	28	" 1871	Watson LEWIS J.P.
59.	Sterting FAGANS	Emma LITTLETON	Henry FAGANS	Amanda FAGANS	Jerry LITTLETON	Tobitha LITTLETON	Merry Hill	28	" 1871	ThaddeusWILSON Bap.Min
60.	William SMITH	Elizabeth SMITHWICK	Granville SMITH	Nancy SMITH	Jonathan SKILES	Hasty SMITHWICK	Windsor	28	" 1871	Henry G COOPER J.P.
61.	Jordan BOND	Martha WILSON	Jordan MORING	Mary WEBB	Unknown	Lucky WILSON	"	28	" 1871	J W COMPTON Metht.Min.
62.	Abram OUTLAW	Lydia CREASY	Simon OUTLAW	Leah OUTLAW	Jack CREASY	Lucy CREASY	Merry Hill	30	" 1871	ThaddeusWILSON Bap.Min
63.	Henry WHITE	Celia WHITE	Jacob WHITE	Harriet WHITE	Harry MORRISS	Louiza WHITE	Colerain	30	" 1871	J. W. SESSOMS J. P.
64.	George HYMAN	Harriet BOND	Jordan HYMAN	Rosetta HARRELL	John HUGER	Annie BOND	Windsor	2d.	Jan. 1872	Wm WALTON JP
65.	John T DEMPSEY	Mary DEMPSEY	James DEMPSY	Anna DEMPSY	Dossey DEMPSEY	Mary DEMPSY	Merry Hill	4	" 1872	Edward PEARCE Bap.Min.
66.	Moses BOON	Rose RUFFIN	Henry VEALE	Viney BOON	Harriss RUFFIN	Marina RUFFIN	Roxobel	4	" 1872	Bryant LEE Bap. Min
67.	Robbin SPIVEY	Fannie RASCOE	Thompson SPIVEY	Mariah SPIVEY	Hosea PUGH	Alsey PUGH	Windsor	4	" 1872.	Wm WALTON J. P.
68.	Albert CARTER	Rachel SMALLWOOD	Moses GILLAM	Mariah CARTER	James SMALLWOOD	Renda SMALLWOOD	"	4	" 1872	" " J. P.
69.	Luke SMALLWOOD	Polly RUFFIN	Robbin PUGH	Lucky RUFFIN	Robert MASON	Mary Ann PUTNEY	"	6	" 1872	Jerry BUNCH Bap. Min.
70.	Henry BRIDGER	Hellen JONES	Frank CORBET	Judy BRIDGERS	Britton JONES	Isabella JONES	"	6	" 1872	" " "
71.	Levi CLARK	Clarra SUTTON	Thomas CLARK	Unknown	Unknown	Nelly SUTTON	Woodville	6	" 1872	Watson LEWIS J.P.

1871/1872

(51) 9 Marriage Register.

Name of Male.	Name of Female.	Name of Father of Male.	Name of Mother of Male.	Name of Father of Female.	Name of Mother of Female.	Place of Marriage.	When Married.		By Whom Married
72. Wm. R BLACKSTON	Henrietta PARKER	Thomas H BLACKSTON	Elizabeth BLACKSTON	John PARKER	Emily PARKER	Snakebite Twp.	9 January	1872	Jeremiah BUNCH Bap.Min
73. Jos. A ROBERTSON	Miss Sawyer WARD	William ROBERTSON	Martha ROBERTSON	Dembry WARD	Sallie WARD	Windsor	" 11	1872	" " "
74. Jackson MITCHELL	Ellen CHERRY	Dossey MITCHELL	Winnie MITCHELL	Ned NYMNS	Petina MITCHELL	Mitchells	" 11	1872	A. JENKINS J.P.
75. Luther R TYLER	Miss Sue CAPEHART	Perry C TYLER	Celia TYLER	Wm. J CAPEHART	Eliza CAPEHART	Roxobel	" 11	1872	Jos. LEUS? Meth.Minis.
76. George WHITE	Roxana EASON	George PERVIS	Rachel BLANCHARD	George EASON	Mary EASON	Snakebite	" 13	1872	Bryant LEE Bap.Ministt.
77. Turner THOMPSON	Martha RUFFIN	Titus THOMPSON	Unknown	Daniel RUFFIN	Lavina WILIBER?	Roxobel	" 13	1872	" " "
78. John T BOND	Miss Pattie WILLIAMS	James BOND	Harriet BOND	John WILLIAMS	Harriet WILLIAMS	Snakebite	" 14	1872	Jeremiah BUNCH Bap.Min.
79. Marsh PUGH	June RASCOE	Abram PUGH	Peggy PUGH	Daniel RASCOE	Cody RASCOE	Windsor	" 16	1872	Wm WALTON J.P.
80. Thomas CAMPBELL	Hetty RASCOE	Unknown	Charles? CAMPBELL	Arthur RASCOE	Norras RASCOE	"	" 16	1872	" "
81. Harrison WHITE	Miss Bettie WHITE	Harrison WHITE	Tempy WHITE	Medea WHITE	Martha WHITE	Whites	" 18	1872	George W COBB "
82. John W SMITHWICK	Miss Ida HYMAN	Samuel SMITHWICK	Martha A SMITHWICK	William HYMAN	Martha J HYMAN	Windsor	" 18	1872	J.W.COMPTON Metht.Min.
83. Dean JONES	Margaret RUFFIN	Miles JONES	Tatty BOND	Unknown	Patsy RUFFIN	"	" 20	1872	Abram MEBANE Bap.Min.
84. Wm. Alpheus LAWRANCE	Miss Penelope RHODES	Abner LAWRENCE	Martha A LAWRENCE	Wm. G. RHODES	Elizabeth RHODES	"	" 23	1872	David HARRELL Bap.Min.
85. Thomas COFFIELD	Miss Margaret NEWBERN	Luke COFFIELD	Elizabeth COFFIELD	John NEWBERN	Unknown	Whites	" 26	1872	George COBB J.P.
86. Thomas BURDEN	Rebecca MITCHELL	Dick JENKINS	Emma BURDEN	Sip MITCHELL	Hannah MITCHELL	Snakebite	" 27	1872	Thos. W SKIRVIN J.P.
87. Jacob MOORE	Dicy ARMSTEAD	Maken MOORE	Anney MOORE	Simon ARMSTEAD	Bettie ARMSTEAD	Merry Hill	" 27	1872	Thaddeus WILSON Bap.Min.
88. Mills SPELLER	Penny MASON	Wright SPELLER	Violet WIGGINS	Henry MASON	Abby MASON	Windsor	" 1	Feb. 1872	Edd. WOOTEN Episl.Minis
89. Thomas PEELE	Dolly JOHNSON	Ned PEELE	Rose PEELE	Daniel JOHNSON	Plesant JOHNSON	Woodvill	" 3	1872	Bryant LEE.Bap. Minis
90. Thomas J HARRELL	Avarilla MIZELL	David HARRELL	Lucy E HARRELL	Moses L MIZELL	Mary MIZELL	Windsor	" 4	1872	Edwd.WOOTEN Epis.Minis
91. Warren GILLAM	Lovey DEMPSY	Guye GILLAM	Rachel GILLAM	Jackson DEMPSEY	Serapan DEMPSY	Merry Hill	" 5	1872	Thaddeus WILSON Bap.Min.
92. James T. MC DANIEL	Miss Patsy J. CULIPHER	James MC DANIEL	Orpy MC DANIEL	Simon CULIPHER	Fannie CULIPHER	" "	" 8	1872	J. W. SMITH J.P
93. James E HUGHES	Miss Mary DAVIS	James HUGHES	Sarah HUGHES	Aaron DAVIS	Nancy DAVIS	Windsor	" 14	1872	Jeremiah BUNCH B. Min
94. Daniel SMALLWOOD	Gracy BOND	Knowledge PUGH	Milly SMALLWOOD	Dennis BOND	Laura BLOUNT	Woodville	" 15	1872	Wm. WALTON J.P.
95. Henry C ALGER	Sarah E. WHITAKER	Henry ALGER	(blank) ALGER	(blank) WHITAKER	(blank)	Windsor	" 15	1872	Jas. W COMPTON Meth.Min.
96. William H. HARRELL	Miss Nancy C. BROWN	Noah HARRELL	Mary HARRELL	Thomas W BROWN	Penelope BROWN	Colerain	" 15	1872	John W SESSOMS J.P.
97. Benjn. LEE	Hasty BURDEN	Bryant LEE	(blank)	Ben MITCHELL	Hester BURDEN	Snakebite	" 15	1872	Bryant LEE Bap. Min.
98. Dempsy BOND	Jane GROVES	Harry BOND	Flinnie BOND	Not known	Not known	Windsor	" 17	1872	Abram MEBANE Bap. Min.
99. Joseph CHERRY	Eady RASCOE	Noah CHERRY	Tempy CHERRY	Antony RASCOE	Notice RASCOE	"	" 25	1872	Wm. WALTON J.P.
100.Hill CHERRY Jr	Lucinda CHERRY	Hill CHERRY	Lizina CHERRY	Benjn. CHERRY	Emeline CHERRY	"	" 5	Mar. 1872	Bryant LEE Bap.Minister
101.Lorenza SMALLWOOD	Margaret SMALLWOOD	Moses SMALLWOOD	Martilla SMALLWOOD	Frank SMALLWOOD	Eady SMALLWOOD	"	" 15	1872	Ed. WOOTEN Epis. Minis

(52) 10 Marriage Register.

Name of Male.	Name of Female.	Name of Father of Male.	Name of Mother of Male.	Name of Father of Female.	Name of Mother of Female.	Place of Marriage.	When Married.			By Whom Married
102.Daniel COOPER	Balinda STEPHENSON	Not known	Adaline COOPER	Mat GILLAM	Clora WARD	Windsor Twp.	1	April	1872	Bryant LEE Bap. Minis
103.Ned WATSON	Lucy BAZEMORE	Hanabell MILLER	Marrah WATSON	Peter BAZEMORE	Caroline BAZEMORE	Snakebite "	1	"	1872	" " " "
104.Wm. W. CLARK	Violet BOND	Frank CLARK	Louisa CLARK	Dick BOND	Delia BOND	Woodville "	6	"	1872	Wm WALTON J.P.
105.Washington RUFFIN	Mary John HARDY	Abram BOYKIN	Milly RUFFIN	Alfred HARDY	Winnie HARDIE	" "	13	"	1872	Watson LEWIS J.P.
106.Littleton T. WARD	Roxana CASPER	Starky WARD	Fannie WARD	Wm. CASPER Sr	Margaret CASPER	Snakebite "	18	"	1872	Jeremiah BUNCH Bap.Min.
107.George COOPER	Notice BOND	King COOPER	Edward COOPER	Dennis BOND	Jenny BOND	Windsor "	20	"	1872	Abram NEBANE Bap. Min.
108.Solomon CARTER	Caroline JORDAN	Solomon SPIVEY	Sarah SPIVEY	Solomon SWAIN	Not known	" "	21	"	1872	John G MITCHELL J.P.
109.Armstead WYNNS	Lizzie BOND	Gilbert NICHOLLS	Penny WYNNS	David BOND	Rhoda BOND	Colerain "	4	Jan.	"	B B WILLIAMS Bap. Min
110.Jacob HOLLOMON	Yuritha C THOMPSON	William HOLLOMON	Priscilla HOLLOMON	James THOMPSON	Rachel THOMPSON	" "	11	"	"	" " " "
111.Munroe RICE	Lucinda WYNNS	Chance TAYLOE	Jane TAYLOE	Not known	Deliala WYNNS	Windsor "	18	"	"	" " " "
112.John A OUTLAW	Miss M. J. MATTHEWS	Alexander OUTLAW	Kiddy OUTLAW	Jacob O MATTHEWS	Sallie MATTHEWS	Colerain "	1	Feb.	"	" " " "
113.James P BELICH	Frances J HOLLOMON	William BELICH	Nancy BELICH	David HOLLOMON	Jane HOLLOMON	" "	8	"	"	" " " "
114.Benjn. POOL	Alice COSTIN	Toney NEBANE	Chovey NEBANE	Not known	Cary COSTIN	White's "	3	Mar.	"	G. W. COBB J. P.
115.Willy GREEN	Gilly PUGH	George GREEN	Jenny GREEN	Silas PUGH	Mariney? PUGH	Woodville "	16	"	"	Benjn. CLARK Bap.Min.
116.Wm. J. R. BROWN	Sarah E. LEWIS	Not known	Catherine HARRELL	Not known	Not known	Merry Hill"	17	"	"	J. W. SMITH J. P.
117.Agustus HUGHES	Mary FREEMAN	James HUGHES	Sarah HUGHES	John FREEMAN	Mary FREEMAN	White's "	20	"	"	Geo. W. COBB J. P.
118.John HILL	Fannie SPELLER	Austin HULL	Cherry MOORE			Windsor "	28	"	"	John G MITCHELL J.P.
119.Bryant MITCHELL	Amy WARD	Ben MITCHELL	Cherry MITCHELL	Frank WARD	Naura WARD	" "	2	April	"	" " " "
120.Charles H. WILLIAMS	Harriet A. WILDER	Cornelius WILLIAMS	Ann WILLIAMS	Mitchell WILDER	Mary WILDER	Colerain "	14	"	"	J. W. SESSOMS
121.Guye WILLIAMS	Annie SMALLWOOD	Lewis WILLIAMS	Phillis WILLIAMS	Cato THOMPSON	Lizzina SMALLWOOD	Woodville "	29	"	"	Wm. WALTON
122.Julius MORING	Lizzie HOGGARD	Zed MORING	Carry MORING	Calvin HOGGARD	Jennet HOGGARD	Windsor "	4	May	"	H C. COOPER
123.Cain ELLIS	Louisa LEE	Not known	Not known	James LEE	Olive LEE	(blank) "	11	"	"	Watson LEWIS
124.Jacob CHAMBLY	Mary CHAMBLY	Willis CHAMBLY	Martha CHAMBLY	Joseph CHAMBLY	Rose CHAMBLY	Colerain "	12	"	"	G. N. GREEN
125.Augustus DONALDSON	Amanda A POWELL	William CASPER	Margaret DONALDSON	Richard POWELL	Mary POWELL	Snakebite "	17	"	"	Jereh.BUNCH,Bap.Min.
126.John RASCOE	Nancy JAMES	William RASCOE	Lucy BREMBRY	Anthony JAMES	Nancy JAMES	Merry-Hill"	18	"	"	Thaddeus WILSON " "
127.Abel HUSON	Susan R WILLIAMS	John HUSON	Elizabeth HUSON	Charles WILLIAMS	Elizabeth WILLIAMS	Colerain "	19	"	"	B B WILLIAMS " "
128.Freeman EVANS	Almira WHITE	Freeman EVANS	Celia EVANS	James WHITE	Sallie WHITE	" "	19	"	"	" " " "
129.Daniel READY	Mahala WILLIAMS	Dempsy READY	Celia W. SPIVEY	Ned WILLIAMS	Aggy WILLIAMS	Merry-Hill"	25	"	"	Thaddeus WILSON " "
130.Wm. Richard COOPER	Mary A PHELPS	Asa COOPER	Lizzie COOPER	William PHELPS	Mary PHELPS	" "	30	"	"	Edd. PEARCE " "
131.Aaron L. COLLINS	Amanda R BAZEMORE	William COLLINS	Elizabeth COLLINS	Abisha BAZEMORE	Fannie BAZEMORE	Windsor"	(blank)		"	Jereh. BUNCH " "

1872

1872

(53) 11 Marriage Register.

Name of Male.	Name of Female.	Name of Father of Male.	Name of Mother of Male.	Name of Father of Female.	Name of Mother of Female.	Place of Marriage.	When Married.	By Whom Married
132.John FREEMAN	Malviny VALENTINE	Samuel FREEMAN	Winney FREEMAN	Isaac OUTLAW	Bettie OUTLAW	Colerain Twp.	Jan. 7th. 1872	Emanuel RENOLDS BapMin.
133.William COLLINS	Lovey LANGDALE	Dick WATSON	Letty COOPER	Miles BAYLEY	Hannah LANGDALE	Merry Hill	June 9th.	H. C. COOPER J. P.
134.James R LAWRENCE	Sallie RAYE===	Levi LAWRENCE===	Sallie LAWRENCE	Jacob RAYE	Penny RAYE	"	" 13.	J. W. SMITH "
135.Axam CAPEHART	Mariah SPRUELL	Abner SIKES	Eliza SYKES	David SPRUELL	Nicie SPRUELL	Roxobel	" 15.	Benjn. Clark Bap. Min.
136.Jefferson SUTTON	Caroline WILLIAMS	Henry OUTLAW	Margaret SUTTON	Alfred WILLIAMS	Joanna WILLIAMS	Windsor	" 22.	Bryant LEE "
137.William BOND	Frances LAWRENCE	Silas BOND	Rebeaca BOND	Robert LAWRENCE	Sallie Ann LAWRENCE	"	" 27.	David HARRELL "

END

GROOM INDEX

-A-

ACRE
Wm. A. 12
ADKISSON
Stephen 45
ALAXANDER
Robert G. 2
ALEN
____ 38
ALGER
Henry C. 51
ALLEN
John 46
ANDERSON
Henry 35
ARMISTEAD
Jerry 41
ASKEW
Aaron O. 28
Eli 46
H. W. 44
Henry 9
Isaac 44
Richard W. 37
Thos. 29
William P. 27
William W. 10

-B-

BACKUS
Madison 45
BAKER
George 27
John 43
Wm. W. 16
BARNACASLE
Jas. H. 49
BARNHILL
Edward 47
BARRETT
M. E. G. 21
BARROW
Knowledge 48
BASNETT
Jack 1
Thomas 21
BAZEMOR
____ 25
BAZEMORE
James G. 25
James R. 37
Jos. W. 48
Joseph 48
Lewis 43
Nelson 32
Peter F. 23
Winston 34
BELICH
James P. 52
BELL
William 12,38
BERNARD
Andrew 18
BIRD
William D. 50
Wm. G. 20
BISHOP
Richard 35
BLACKSTON
Wm. R. 51
BLOUNT
John 47
BOND
Abram 28
Bob 24
David 48
Dempsy 51

BOND (Cont.)
George 43
Isaac 44
John T. 51
Jordan 50
Joseph 28
Miles 10
Neptan 35
Stewart 34
Thomas 33
Washington 26
William 53
BONNER
Thomas 24
BOOKER
George 47
BOON
Harry 23
Moses 50
BOSKY
Joseph 48
BOWEN
Marcus H. 40
BOWZER
Henry A. 13
BRICKEL
James D. 49
BRIDGER
Henry 50
Justin 34
BRIGGS
Willis 28
BRIMAGE
____ 8
BRITTON
Auntny L. 21
Daniel W. 10
BROWN
George 26
Henderson 26
Henry 7
James 26
Nero 43
Robert R. 22
Thos. W. 41
Washington 7
William H. 44
Wm. J. R. 52
BRYANT
Alfred 38
BUNCH
Frederic 47
Henry 25
James 36
John 48
Jos. W. 1
Wm. H. 32
BURDEN
George A. 3
Madison 33
Thomas 51
BURRESS
Joseph Joseph J. 8
BURROWO
T. A. 47
BUSH
Robert 16
BUTLER
Harvey 29
BYRUM
Daniel E. 38
James H. 19

-C-

CAMPBELL
Thomas 51
CAPEHART

CAPEHART (Cont.)
Axam 53
Cademus 2
Wm. A. 7
Wm. E. 39
CAPHART
____ 7
CARTER
Albert 50
Peter 45
Robert 48
Solomon 52
Washington 44
CASPER
Arter 20
George M. 48
William 11
William A. 50
William J. 49
CASTELLOW
Hill J. 49
John D. 46
CHAMBLY
Jacob 52
CHERRY
Arter 12
Ben 7
George 16,45
Henry 33
Hill, Jr. 51
Jo 44
Joseph 51
Noah 2
Wright 24
CHURCHWELL
William J. 3
CLABON
Peter 13
CLARK
Cubit 44
Frank 33,50
Freeman 44
George 3,21
Harry 31
Henry 3
Jessee 44
John 46
King L. 44
Levi 50
Thomas 43
Wm. W. 52
COBB
Shadrick 48
Turner 49
COFFIELD
A. J. 45
R. W. 47
Ruffin 15
Thomas 51
COGGAN
Wm. G. 47
COGGINS
Robert 27
COLLINS
Aaron L. 52
Prince A. 1
William 53
CONNER
Joseph 14
COOPER
Armstead 48
Daniel 52
George 31,52
George A. 46
Haywood 36
Wm. Richard 52
COX
Richard 45
CRAIG

CRAIG (Cont.)
Andrew 50

-D-

DANALDS
____ 35
DANIEL
Ezekiel 46
DAVIDSON
George M. 22
DAVIS
Allen, Jr. 9
DEMPSEY
John T. 50
DEMPSY
Amariah 48
Augustus 47
DEVEREAUX
Essex 17
DICKSON
James 43
DONALD
Giles 35
DONALDSON
Augustus 52
Isaiah 49
DOUGLAS
Lewis 49
DOWNING
George W. 22
DUNDALOW
Henry 43
DUNNING
Jessee 15
Willie J. 43
DUNSTAN
____ 10
DUNSTON
H. V. 10

-E-

ELLIS
Cain 52
ELLYSON
Washington 32
EPPS
Harry 31
EURE
Mills 28
EVANS
Aaron J. 17
Freeman 52
George E. 45
Ishniel 26
James H. 6
Joseph D. 46
Thomas P. 41
Thomas Payton 43
Yancy 47
EVERETT
Zarra 32

-F-

FAGANS
Sterting 50
FIELDS
Andrew 33
FRANKS
Alfred 5
FREEMAN
Bill 44
John 53
Ned 30
FULCHER
Carson 44

-G-

GARRETT
Abram 11
GASKINS
Clark 48
GILLAM
Allen 45
Armistead 30
Ceasor 46
Frederick 11
Turner 3
Warren 51
Willis 24
GORDEN
William 47
GRAY
Benjamin 28
Maderson 32
Thomas 7
Thompson 48
GREEN
Willy 52
GREGORY
Hubbard 2
GRIFFIN
Dick 43
John L. 47
GURGANOUS
Henry S. 17

-H-

HALL
Gustavus P. 45
HARDY
Jas. 1
Joseph H. 14
HARE
Starkey 38
HARGRAVE
Wm. 47
HARRELL
Antony 37
D. C. 12
George B. 7
James H. 46
John B. 14
Jos. J. 8
Thomas J. 51
William H. 51
HARRISON
Kader 12
HARRISS
Richard 40
HAYS
Peter 45
HECKSTALL
Ceasor 44
Isaac 44
HENDRICKS
John 11
HENDRIX
Starky 44
HENRY
Reddick 37
HILL
George 46
James 12
John 52
Nead 7
Neal 7
HOBBS
Charles C. 4
George W. 46
HOGGARD
____ 8
George W. 49
John 46

HOGGARD (Cont.)
    John D.   25
    Moses   45
HOGGAR
    Abel   8
HOLLAND
    Jacob   45
HOLLEY
    Charles   45
    Ellick   9
    Hunter   16
    Nead   29
    Thos. D.   8
HOLLOMON
    Jacob   52
    Samuel   43
HOWARD
    Reddick H. 35
HOWELL
    Henry W.   34
HUGHES
    Agustus   52
    James E.   51
HUGHS
    John   45
HUNT
    Thomas   49
HUSON
    Abel   52
HYMAN
    George   50
    Harry   40
    London   45

-I-

None

-J-

JACKSON
    Thomas J. 39
JACOCKS
    Jonathan J. 22
JENKINS
    Charles S. 49
    Henry   46
    Joseph W. 43
JERNIGAN
    Augustus   50
    George   47
    James R.   10
    John H.   44
    Nathaniel 12
    Starkey   25
JOHNSON
    Dallis   18
    Jacob   45
    James   46
    James P.   3
    John W.   13
    Joseph   46
    Turner   41
JONES
    Alexander 49
    Dean   51
    Eli   20
    George   49
    James   47
    Peyton   19
    Simon   17
    Willis   15
JORDEN
    Rollen   43
JOYNER
    ----   40

-K-

KENIDY
    Joseph D. 50
KNOWLES
    John E.   39

-L-

LANGLEY
    James W.   47
LASSITER
    Jessee   14
LAW

LAW (Cont.)
    Lazarus   20
LAWRANCE
    Wm. Alpheus 51
LAWRENCE
    James R.   53
    Jeremiah   24
    Robert   39
LEARRY
    Benja.   17
    Henry   11
    Simon   17
LEARY
    William F. 44
LEE
    Anthony   23
    Benjn.   51
    George W. 36
    Jack   29
    James   43
    John   36
    Moses   22
    Peter   45
    Robt.   13
LEGGETT
    William   45
LINCH
    Henry   3
LIVERMAN
    James H.   6
LOW
    John   2
LUCESTER
    Jonathan   23

-M-

MC.GLAUHON
    Alfred   44
MC DANIEL
    James T.   51
MC DERMITT
    Jessee   30
MANNING
    Joseph   30
MARTIN
    James   41
MASON
    Charles   47
MEBANE
    Joseph   14
MILES
    J. W.   46
MILLER
    Frank   14
    Solomon   43
    West   49
MITCHELL
    Abbiat   9
    Alfred   46
    Bryant   52
    Darious R. 46
    F. V.   33
    George   34
    J. W.   41
    Jackson   51
    James E.   19
    Rufus   21
    Silas   44
    Thomas M.   5
    Watson   49
MIZELL
    George   10
    Henry   49
    John   37
    Mathew H. 26
    Starkey E. 31
    Thadeus   30
    William   15
MODLIN
    Joseph   4
MOORE
    Jacob   51
    Sandy   49
MORING
    Joseph   37
    Julius   52
MORRISS
    Allen   39
    Calvin J. 48
    Gaston H. 46

MORRISS (Cont.)
    Hinton   50
    James, Sr. 16
    M. B.   20
MYERS
    Isaac   13
    Ralph   32

-N-

NICHOLLS
    Jefferson 49
    Thos. L.   4
NORFLEET
    Anthony   42,43
    Richmond   40

-O-

ODOM
    Isum   30
OUTLAW
    Abram   50
    Alfred   3
    Britton   18
    Harry   45
    John A.   52
    Joseph W.   9
    Oscar   39
    Primas   44
    William   2

-P-

PAGE
    George   33
    Soloman   34
PARKER
    Fred   7
    James B.   31
    Jos. S.   49
    Thomas H. 45
    William D. 44
PEARCE (See also
PIERCE)
    Edward   47
    Jos. P.   48
    Wright   48
PEEBLES
    Peter   29
PEEL
    Geo. T.   15
    J. T.   18
PEELE
    Drew   28
    Rubin J.   14
    Thomas   51
PENDER
    Morriss   4
PERRY
    Bryant   49
    Charles   16
    Elisha   5
    Frank   15
    George P. 50
    William W. 23
    Wm. T.   44
PHELPS
    Henry   43
PIERCE (See also
PEARCE)
    James K.   35
PITT
    B. F.   11
POOL
    Ben   41,43
    Benjn.   52
POWELL
    John   48
    Lewis   38
    Simon   6
PRICE
    Ebenezer   47
PRITCHARD
    A. J.   32
    Docton   36
PRUDEN
    Alfred   44
PUGH
    Daniel   27
    David   23

PUGH (Cont.)
    Guye   46
    Marsh   51
    Outlaw   49
    William   46

-Q-

None

-R-

RANKINS
    Jordan   25
RASCOE
    Britton   30
    Hardy   47
    John   52
    Primos   47
RAWLES
    James H.   9
RAYFORD
    Frank   44
RAYNER
    Blount   45
    Noah   37
    Wright   4
READY
    Daniel   52
REED
    Robert   2
RHODES
    Solomon   49
    Thomas J. 33
RICE
    Daniel   26
    Munroe   52
    York   44
ROBBINS
    Daniel   45
    Samuel   1
    Slade   50
ROBERTSON
    Jos. A.   51
ROBINSON
    James   46
ROGERS
    Jacob   50
RUFFIN
    Abner   5
    Ephraim   48
    Hilard   6
    Jessee   8
    Minor   20
    Noah   39
    Simon   43
    Stephen   44
    Washington 52

-S-

SANDERLIN
    Wm. A.   46
SANDERS
    James E.   1
SAVAGE
    Henry   36
SCOTT
    Cater   29
SESSOMS
    Andrew   49
    D. V.   21
    Preston H. 19
    Tony   24
SHARP
    George   2
SHAW
    George W. 40
    William T. 45
SHERROD
    Jessee   43
SIMMONS
    Caeser   31
SINGLETON
    Frank   47
SLURGE
    Harry   35
SMALL
    Isaac   43
SMALLWOOD
    Benjamin   17

SMALLWOOD (Cont.)
    Cesar   50
    Daniel   51
    J. R.   15
    Lorenza   51
    Luke   50
    Madison   48
    Noah   22
    Prince   34
    Robert   48
    Solomon   28
SMITH
    Chas.   19
    John W.   50
    Stephen   23
    Thomas   46
    Turner   7
    William   50 (2)
SMITHWICK
    John W.   51
    Thos.   49
SPELLER
    David   47
    Mills   51
    Rubin   27
    Sollomon   4
SPIVEY
    George   20
    Lewis   45
    Robbin   50
    Robert   45
SPRUILL
    J. R. H.   27
STEPHENSON
    Daniel   43
    Edward   48
STEWART
    Charles   36
STONE
    John   29
SUTTON
    Jefferson 53
    Jessee   18
    Lewis B.   19
    Wm. M.   19

-T-

TADLOCK
    Peter   13
TASWELL
    William   49
TAYLOE
    Aquilla   31
    George   48
    Henry   9
TAYLOR
    William   47
THOMAS
    Blount   47
    John H.   47
    Joseph J. 43
THOMPSON
    Aaron   43
    Friley   35
    George   11
    Hampton   34
    Isom   46
    Joseph   46
    Nathan   46
    Nelson   27
    Turner   51
    Willis   47
    Wm. S.   10
    Worter   29
TILLARY
    William   42
TILLERRY
    William   43
TODD
    A. C.   44
    Jacob W.   49
    James S.   48
    Korly   6
TREADWELL
    ----   25
TREDWELL
    Drew   25
TREVATHAN
    James E.   50
TURPIN

TURPIN (Cont.)
  Henry 48
TYLER
  Luther R. 51

-U-

URQUHART
  Alfred Slade 5
  Burges 47
  Wiley 6

-V-

VALENTINE
  Thomas 45
VICK
  Wm. H. 12

-W-

WADKINS
  Albert 43
WALKER
  Abbert 43
  Benjn. M. 49
WALTON
  David 18
  Meridy 18
WARD
  George D. 5
  Joseph W. 14
  Littleton T. 52
WARSAW
  Peter 6
WATFORD
  Daniel 32
  Henry 25
  William Ben 16
WATSON
  Charles 45
  George 44
  Joseph 45
  Ned 52
  Shadrick 15,46
WATTS
  John 16
WEBB
  William 47
WEED
  Marcus A. 4
WEST
  Cisaro 50
WHITE
  Alfred 43
  Arter 24
  Ben 30
  Daniel W. 47
  Drew 43
  George 51
  George W. 50
  Harrison 51
  Haywood 23
  Henry 48,50
  John 18
  Joseph A. 4
  Joseph J. 44
  Joseph W. 43
  Kenneth 31,48
  Manassa 19
  Watson L. 25
  Wm. T. 46
WHITUS
  Ned 45
WILKINS
  Henry 5,46,49
WILLIAMS
  Abert 13
  Abram 47
  Charles H. 37,52
  Docton 22
  Guye 52
  Hampton 21
  Harry 11
  Jefferson 49
  Nelson 17,21
  Peter 6
  Richard 5
  Samuel 8
  Sandy 1
  Soloman 27

WILLIAMS (Cont.)
  Thomas 14
  Vanburin 26
  Willie 44
WILLIFORD
  Joseph W. 40
WILLOUGHBY
  Spencer 22
WILNEY
  Owen 10
WILSON
  Andrew 38
  Thomas 36
WINBON
  ____ 8
WINBONE
  John Henry 8
WINTON
  Robert 38
WOOD
  Mirabana L. 45
  Trim 49
WOOTTEN
  Edwd. 49
WORTHINGTON
  Dennison 50
WYNN
  Granville 20
WYNNS
  Armstead 52
  York 24

-X-

None

-Y-

None

-Z-

None

BRIDE INDEX

-A-

ALLEN
 Precilla 41
AMBERS
 Elizabeth 43
ARMSTEAD
 Dicy 51
ASBEL
 Marinda A. 30
ASKEW
 Alice 43
 Caroline 7
 R. E. 5
 Renda 2
 Rose 39

-B-

BACCHUS
 Alice 5
 Patsey 4
BACCUS
 ---- 5
 Lydia 1
BACKUS
 Penicy 27
BALLANCE
 Elcy 46
BANZORA
 ---- 25
BARNACASCLE
 Ann 47
BARRETT
 Ann E. 12
BAZEMORE
 Amanda R. 52
 Caroline 45
 Emeline 43
 Fabra 46
 Isabell 11
 Isabella 34
 Lucy 52
 Mary E. 31,50
 Sallie Ann 32
 Sarah F. 14
BEASLEY
 Missouri 44
BEASLY
 Annie E. 19
 Mariah 23
BELL
 Everline 13
 Lizzie 40
 Pennie 10
BENNETT
 Esther 32
 Marinda 23
BERNARD
 B. W. 11
BIGGS
 Clara 44
BIRD
 Celia E. 27
 Sarah E. 50
BISHOP
 Julia 16
 Leroy E. 14
BLOUNT
 Clara J. 39
BOND
 Albina 3
 Ann 48
 Annis 47
 Caroline 28
 Elizabeth 13
 Flora 46
 Gracy 51
 Harriet 50

BOND (Cont.)
 Henrietta 36
 Katie 20
 Lizzie 52
 Margaret 28
 Martha 48
 Mary 44,45
 Mary Elizabeth 44
 Notice 52
 Penny 23
 Rosetta 11
 Silva 46
 Susan 26
 Violet 52
 Zilpha 48
BOON
 Mary Ann 46
BOWEN
 Sallie M. 40
BOYKIN
 Harriet E. 39
BRITT
 Adeline P. 22
BROWN
 Agness 31
 Cinaha 43
 Emma 47
 Fillis 18
 Nancy 48
 Nancy C. 51
BRYANT
 Nancy 25
BUNCH
 Bitsy 35
 Louisa 44
BURDEN
 Hasty 51
 Muriah 45
BUTLER
 Celia E. 50
 Eliza J. 9
 Jane 48
 Judy 16
 Margaret 39
 Martha C. 36
 Nancy E. 16
 Victoria 12
BUTT
 Francis A. 25
BUTTER
 Eliza J. 9

-C-

CAPEHART
 Amy 44
 Celia 1
 Julia A. 3
 Mary 49
 Mary E. 33
 Mary M. 2
 S. E. 27
 Sue 51
CASPER
 Harriett 23
 Jane 25
 Nancy 48
 Roxana 52
CASTELLOW
 Joanna 50
CHAMBLY
 Cealy A. 11
 Mary 52
CHERRY
 Becka 29
 Caroline 22
 Elizabeth 48
 Ellen 51

CHERRY (Cont.)
 Ester 34
 Feriby 7
 Foriby 44
 Jane 44,48
 Jane O. 28
 Lucinda 51
 Rebecca 16
 Rose A. 2
 Rose 13
 Sarah 33
 Tempy 30
CLARK
 Adaline 50
 Annice 33
 Chaney 14
 Lidia 38
 Mariah 46
 Mouring 12
 Sarah 46
COBB
 Ceneth P. 37
 Marina 14
COFFIELD
 Gilla 48
 Henrietta 43
COLLINS
 Elizabeth F. 19
 Louisa 18
CONNER
 Elizabeth 30
COOPER
 Adaline 49
 Aggy 47
 Henrietha 37
 Martha 43
 William Ann 48
COSLY
 Adaline 43
COSTAN
 Sallie 38
COSTIN
 Alice 52
COTTON
 Margaret A. 45
COWAND
 Harriet 42,43
COX
 Ellen 7
 Mary L. 12
 Mary M. 49
 Mary S. 12
CREASEY
 Olley 41
CREASY
 ---- 41
 Lydia 50
CULIPHER
 Patsy J. 51
CULLIPHER
 Rebecca 50

-D-

DANIEL
 Basha 6
DAVIS
 Levinia 30
 Martha 45
 Mary 51
DEAM
 Mariah 21
DEMPSEY
 Mary 50
DEMPSY
 Lovey 51
DEVEREAUX
 Chana 40
DONALDSON

DONALDSON (Cont.)
 Ann M. 50
DONALSON
 Alexena 44
DUNDALOW
 Mary 12
DUNNING
 Antonetta 46
 Celia A. 48
 Cherry 46
 Elizabeth 49
 Laura J. 28
 Mary E. 22

-E-

EASON
 Amanda 10
 Roxana 51
EICHE
 Sarah 47
EPPS
 Penelopy 46
ETHERIDGE
 Malvina 48
 Morin 26

-F-

FAGANS
 Isabella 49
FANNING
 Martha 47
FLOYD
 Ceaney 10
 Katie E. 43
FRANCIS
 Isabella A. 36
FREEMAN
 Ann 48
 Elenor 46
 Elizabeth C. 9
 Levinia 43
 Mariah 20
 Martha 15,38
 Mary 52
 Nancy 37
 Rachel 26

-G-

GARDNER
 Celia W. 44
GILLAM
 Betsy 44
 Celia 30
 Harriet 19,28
 Malinda 24
 Pattie 50
GORDEN
 Julia 46
GREEN
 Martha 47
GREGORY
 A. E. 44
GRIFFIN
 Jane 18
GROVES
 Jane 51

-H-

HALE
 Martha J. 43
HANCOCK
 Harriet 16
HARDY
 Hester 17
 Hulday 23

HARDY (Cont.)
 Mary 18
 Mary Ann 22
 Mary E. 46
 Mary John 52
HARGROVE
 Fanny 21
HARMAN
 Ann 4
HARRELL
 Ann M. 4
 Clara 9
 Judy 48
 Mary C. 43
 Penelope 48
HARRISON
 Winnie Ann 46
HECKSTALL
 Jane 38
HENRY
 Henrietta M. 40
HENTON
 Mariah A. 46
HILL
 Alice 12
 Gracy 17
 Mary 4
HINES
 Hannah 5
HODGE
 Laura 50
 Margaret 11
HOGGARD
 Annice 36
 Lizzie 52
 Margaret 18
 Martha 50
 Penelope 21
HOLDER
 Eva 19
 Fannie 1
HOLLEY
 ---- 17
 Caroline 1
 Ellen 14
 Fanny 37
 Malind 4
 Malvina 44
 Patsey 38
 Susan 20
HOLLOMON
 Frances J. 52
 Susan A. 50
HOLLY
 ---- 1
 Ferebee 17
 Priscilla 49
HUGHES
 Celia T. 23
HUGHS
 Elizabeth 44
HYMAN
 Ida 51
 Josephine 34

-I-

None

-J-

JACKSON
 Caroline 25
JAMES
 Mariah 1
 Nancy 52
JENKINS
 Frances 20

JENKINS (Cont.)
  Mary 47
  Mary W. 46
JERNIGAN
  Elizabeth 41, 43
  Mary E. 46
  Sarah 39
JOHNSON
  Dolly 51
  Penelope Ann 49
  Penny 47
JONES
  Arabella 45
  Hellen 50
  Louisa 49
  Patsey 36
JORDAN
  Caroline 52
JOYNER
  Mary 9

-K-

KEETER
  Sallie 47
KING
  Judy 2

-L-

LANE
  Easter 16
  Sara 38
LANGDALE
  Lovey 53
LASITER
  16
LASSITER
  Ida 16
  Rachel 17
LAW
  Mary 49
LAWRENCE
  Frances 53
LEE
  Abby 50
  Delia 53
  Louisa 52
  Martha E. 44
LEWIS
  Sarah E. 52
LITTLETON
  Emma 50
LIVERMAN
  Elizabeth 8
LYNCH
  Francis 27

-M-

MC FARLAND
  Mary 36
MC GLAUHON
  Marinda 35
MC KLEESE
  Margaret 4
MARRISS (See also MORRISS)
  Mary E. 50
MASON
  Penny 51
MATTHEWS
  M. J. 52
MEBANE
  Celia A. 49
  Hasty 49
  Julia M. 50
  Marinda 48
  Mary 9
  Winney 41, 43
  Zilphy 45
MELTON
  Jane 43
MILLER
  Cyntha E. 41
  Julia 8
  Mary E. 10
  Nancy C. 46
  Rebecca 15

MILLER (Cont.)
  Susan 8
MITCHELL
  Alice A. 38
  Rachel 3
  Rebecca 51
  Sarah 49
  Susan C. 18
MIXON
  Mary E. 19
MIZELL
  Avarilla 51
  Fannie 45
  Harriet E. 49
  Jane 11
  Martha 47
  Nicy E. 50
  Rebecca 34
  Sallie 22
MOORE
  Jane 43
  Rachel 49
  Sallie 37
MOORING (See also MORING, MOURNING)
  7
MORGAN
  Jane 47
MORING
  Jane 25
  Venus 49
MORRIS
  Emiline 32
MORRISS (See also MARRISS)
  Ara E. 24
  Belinda 45
  Emaline 25
  Emaline C. 40
  Hester 24
  Mary E. 28
  Nancy E. 15
  Sarah 47
MOURNING
  Cornelia 7
MURRA
  Annie 29
MYERS
  Banzora 25
  Louisa E. 13
  Sallie 19

-N-

NEWBERN
  Margaret 51
NEWSOM
  Fannie M. 48
NICHOLLS
  Bettie 15
  Elizabeth S. 45
  Emily B. 22
  Emma 50
  Lucy 24
NIXON
  Sallie C. 4
NORFLEET
  Harriet 42
  Sarah 47
NOWELL
  Mary E. 10

-O-

OUTLAW
  Jane 45
  Joanna 14
  Kattie 11
  Lucy 17
  Mary 44
  Mary E. 45
  Milly 33
  Penelope 45
  Sarah 46
  Victoria R. 2

-P-

PARKER
  Henrietta 51

PARKER (Cont.)
  Nancy E. 46
  Parthena M. 35
PATTERSON
  Mary 35
PEAARCE
  Jennett 23
PEARCE
  Mary A. 26
PEEL
  Louisa 14
PEELE
  Lucy 45
  Olive 46
PELT
  Hester 45
PERRY
  Celia A. 47, 49
  Emiline 44
  Emma 49
  Laura E. 41
  Margaret 49
  Margaret A. 20
  Martha 21
  Martha E. 48
  Sallie A. 46
PHELPS
  Elizabeth 49
  Henrietta 36
  Joana 49
  Martha R. 45
  Mary A. 52
  R. A. 44
PIERCE
  23
PITMAN
  Mary A. 47
  Virginia C. 22
POWELL
  Adaline 47
  Amand 35
  Amanda A. 52
  Clara 29
  Jennett 45
  Kiddy 14
  Levinia 43
  Mary Ann 6
  Sarah E. 48
PRITCHARD
  R. E. 45
PUGH
  Ann 49
  Cloe 9
  Edie 35
  Gilly 52
  Hannah 47
  Harriet E. 49
  Hasty 32
  Henrietta 17
  Liddy 44
  Mary 2

-Q-

None

-R-

RASCOE
  Cottie 48
  Eady 51
  Fannie 50
  Harriet 29
  Hetty 51
  June 51
  Peggy 43
  Phebee 49
RAY
  Jane 23
RAYE
  Sallie 53
RAYNER
  Bettie 15
  Kary 26
  Martha A. 7
  Mary 47
  Nancy 1
REDDICK
  Mollie 37
REDDITT
  Lucy 18

RHODES
  Alice 49
  Harriet 6, 7
  Mariah 32
  Penelope 51
  Susan M. 39
RICE
  Hettie 21
  Mary E. 8
  Roxanah 43
ROBBINS
  Jane 46
ROSS
  Virginia 47
ROULAC
  Eliza J. 6
ROULHAC
  6
  Jane 47
RUFFIN
  Abby 5
  Amy 44
  Annie D. 15
  Becky 10
  Betsy 44
  Chaney 32
  Dolly 30
  Harriet E. 44
  Jane 46
  Margaret 51
  Martha 51
  Phillis 28
  Polly 46, 50
  Rhoda 8
  Rose 50
  Rosetta 35
  Susan 33
  Winnie 21, 28
RYAN
  Gracy 2
RYON
  Celia 43
  Judy 45

-S-

SADDLER
  Sarah W. 6
SANDERLIN
  Sue 1
SESSOMS
  Mary P. 5
SHARP
  Susan 12
SHARROCK
  Delia 34
SHAW
  Emily C. 45
SHIELDS
  Abba 30
SIMMONS
  Mary D. 43
SKIRVIN
  Susan C. 21
SLAUGHTER
  Jane 3
  Lidia 17
SMALLWOOD
  Anica 29
  Annie 52
  Lizina 22
  Lurinda 34
  Margaret 51
  Mary L. 47
  Rachel 50
  Tempy 24
SMITH
  Bettie 44
  Eva M. 8
  Handy 43
  Sopha 13
SMITHWICK
  Delila 24
  Elizabeth 50
SPELLER
  Fannie 52
  Jane 47
SPIVEY
  Kezziah 45
  Matilda 29
SPRUELL

SPRUELL (Cont.)
  Mariah 53
  Molly 48
SPRUILL
  Sallie 3
STEPHENSON
  Balinda 52
STIONS
  Elizabeth 14
SUTTON
  Clarra 50
  Luvine 29
  Nelly 34
SWAIN
  Eveline 47
  Louisa 6

-T-

TADLOCK
  Mary C. 19
  Prissilla 10
TAYLOE
  Amanda 20
  Belinda 44
  Betsy 27
  Elizabeth 45
  Julia 48
  Julia W. 49
  Lucy 50
  Nancy 26
  Rachel 44
  Ruthy 15
TAYLOR
  Mariah 43
TEAMER
  Ann 45
THOMAS
  Amelia 8
  Patsey 39
  Rose 44
THOMPSON
  Bitsy 13
  Leah 43
  Lizina 31
  Mary B. 47
  Polly 18
  Silvia 41
  Yuritha C. 52
THROWER
  Sarah 15
TODD
  Josephine 31
  Nancy 25
  William A. 45
TREADWELL
  Celia 5
  Leueza 46
  Sarah 7
TYLER
  Aggy 47
  Rachel 5

-U-

URQUHART
  Sylvesta 49

-V-

VALENTINE
  Malviny 53
VEALE
  Rhody 6
VERNOOY
  Leah M. 4
VICK
  Edy 44
  Eliza 48

-W-

WALTON
  Agness 3
  Judy 33
WARD
  Amy 52
  Delia 43
  Emily 27
  Henrietta 32
  Perlina 44

WARD (Cont.)
  Sawyer 51
  Willie A. 46
WATFORD
  Adaline 45
WATSON
  Ann 9
  Emily 43
  Marietta 5
  Muriah 46
  Rosetta 40
  Silva 44
WEBB
  Cherry 47
  Elizabeth 37
  Pelelope 2
WEBSTER
  Mariah 45
WEST
  Mary 26
  Penicy 31
WESTON
  P. E. 9
  Sallie W. 7
WHEELLER
  Sophia 17
WHITAKER
  Mary E. 20
  Sarah E. 51
WHITE
  Almira 52
  Amanda 26
  Ann 30
  Ann Sawyer 49
  Annis 45
  Aritta 12
  Barbary 49
  Bettie 51
  Catharine R. 10
  Celia 50
  Eliza 37
  Emily 47
  Fannie 48
  Fannie E. 46
  Frances 6
  Jane 24
  Kiddy 46
  Levenia 16
  Marinah 29
  Martha E. 3
  Martha J. 31
  Martha W. 19
  Nancy Jane 43
  Narcissa 49
  Priscilla 49
  Susan 24
WIGGINS
  Tempy 38
WILDER
  Harriet A. 52
WILLFORD (See also WILLIFORD)
  Mary Eliza 45
WILLIAMS
  Aniky 44
  Caroline 53
  Cherry 33
  Emaline 31,34
  Hannah 43
  Julia 27
  Louisa 48
  Lucy 45
  Mahala 43,52
  Marenda 21
  Marinda 48
  Mary 20
  Mary C. 45
  Nanny 46
  Pattie 51
  Penny 40
  Rachel 13
  Rhany 8
  Rose 27
  Sallie 33
  Silva 47
  Susan 7
  Susan R. 52
WILLIFORD (See also WILLFORD)
  Jarsey 31
WILSON

WILSON (Cont.)
  Ellen 32
  Malvina 11
  Martha 50
WORLEY
  Chaney 35
WYNN
  ____ 36
  Judy 3
WYNNE
  Annie M. 36
WYNNS
  Frances E. 47
  Lucinda 52

-X-

None

-Y-

None

-Z-

None

GENERAL INDEX

-A-

ADKISON
  Molly 45
ALEMOND
  Jacob 45
ALGER
  ———— 51
  Henry 51
ALLEN
  Jack 46
  Jerry 44
  Rachel 46
AMBERS
  ———— 43
  Henry 43
ARMSTEAD
  Bettie 51
  Simon 51
ASKEW
  Cullen 44
  Isaac 44
  Jenney 44
  Lydia 44
  Rose 43,50
  Rosetta 46

-B-

BACCUS
  Ned 47
BACKUS
  Sarah 45
  Thomas 45
BAKER
  Kizzie 43
  Timothy 43
BALDIN
  Mary 48
BARBER
  B. F. 48
BARNACASCLE
  Geo W. 47,49
  Susan 47
BARNCASCLE
  Susan 49
BARNHILL
  Tincy 47
  Wash 47
BARROW
  Krissy 48
BAWGER
  Henry A. 14
BAYLEY
  Miles 53
BAZEMORE
  Abisha 52
  Aggy 43
  Alder 50
  Caroline 52
  Emeline 50
  Fannie 52
  Fred 45
  Hab 48
  Hannah 46
  John 48
  Penny 48
  Peter 52
  Rebecca 48
  Washington 43
  William 48
BEASLEY
  J. W. 44
  Julia A. 44
BELICH
  Nancy 52
  William 52
BELL
  Freeman 50

BELL (Cont.)
  Mahala 45
BERN
  Eley 46
  Majah 46
BIDDLE
  Vilet 46
BIGGS
  Winnie 44
BIRD
  Caroline 50
  Sarah 50(2)
  Wilie 50(2)
BISHOP
  (George) 45
  George 5 (2),
6(2),7,9,14(3),
15,16(2),18,40,
41,42,43(2),44,
45
  William H. 3
  Wm. H. 3
BLACKSTON
  Elizabeth 51
  Thomas H. 51
BLANCHARD
  Rachel 51
BLOUNT
  Gusther 47
  Katie 47
  Laura 51
BOND
  Annie 50
  Anthony 45
  Bristas 48
  Brister 47
  Cherry 48
  Cloa 46
  Cloe 47
  Daffy 48
  David 52
  Delia 52
  Dennis 51,52
  Dick 52
  Fedrick 48
  Flinnie 51
  Hanna 45
  Harriet 51
  Harry 51
  James 51
  Jane 44(2)
  Jenny 52
  Lewis T. 48
  Mariah 48
  Rebeaca 53
  Rebecca 48
  Rhoda 52
  Sallie 48
  Silas 53
  Tatty 51
  Valdo 48
BOON
  Alaxander 48
  Rindy 46
  Tom 46
  Viney 50
BOYKIN
  Abram 52
BREMBRY
  Lucy 52
BRICKEL
  James 49
  Nancy 49
BRIDGERS
  Judy 50
BRITTON
  Charity 46
BROWN
  Anthony 43

BROWN (Cont.)
  Ben 44
  Benjn. 48
  (George) 45
  Geo. 27,30,
31,35,38,47
  George 18(2),
21(2),27-32,
33(4),34(2),
35(3),38(2),
43(3),44,46(4),
  Gorge 27(2)
  Harriet 43,
45
  Isaac 44
  Nancy 44
  Penelope 51
  Susan 44
  Syntha 48
  Thomas W. 51
  William 45
BUNCH
  Cullen 47
  J. 50(2)
  J. H. 13
  Jereh. 52(2)
  Jeremiah 1,2,
5,9(2),11,12,15,
17-20,22,25,29,
31,32(2),34-36,
39,43(2),44,
45(2),46,47,
48(2),49(2),
51(3),52
  Jerremiah 47
  Jerry 50
  Jessee H. 13,
14
  Moring 44
  Rhoda 47
  Rose 48
  Theophilus 44
BURDEN
  Caroline 43
  Emma 51
  Gracy 45
  Hester 51
  John L. 43
  Lewis 45
BURROW
  John 47
BUTLER
  James 50
  Jane 50

-C-

CALE
  D. 12
  Duncan L. 12
  Penny 50
CAMPBEL
  Charles 51
CAPEHART
  Adaline 49
  Antony 49
  Eliza 51
  Isaac 49
  Sophia 44
  Wm. J. 51
CARTER
  Dicy 44
  Emma 45
  Jana 44
  Mariah 50
  Rebecca 48
  Solomon 43,48
  Thomas 44
CASPER

CASPER (Cont.)
  Jared 48
  Margaret 49,52
  Marina 50
  Mary 48
  Peggy 48
  Thomas 50
  William 48,52
  William J. 49
  Wm., Sr. 52
CASTELLOW
  Henry 50
  Larry 46
  Levi 49
  Patsy 49
  Vallie 46
CHAMBLY
  Joseph 52
  Martha 52
  Rose 52
  Willis 52
CHERRY
  Ann 48
  Ben 44
  Benjn. 51
  Bryant 48
  Emeline 44,51
  Hannah 48
  Hill 44,51
  Levina 45
  Lizina 51
  Mariah 45
  Noah 45(2),51
  Noah, Sr. 45
  Tempy 51
  Zina 44
CLARK
  Ben 31,36,44
  Ben Jamin 13
  Benj. 9,12,44,
46
  Benjaman 40
  Benjamin 7,8,
13-15,17(3),27
  Benjamon 14,40
  Benjmin 17
  Benjn. 43,46,
48,49(2),52,53
  Binjmin 8
  David 48
  Emanuel 46
  Frank 52
  Harklas 50
  Hasty 50
  Hoodus 44
  Jerry 46
  Jubiter 44
  Lara 44
  Lawra 50
  Liss 44
  Louisa 44,52
  Lovey 46
  Martha 43
  Sarah 44
  Thomas 50
  Violet 44
COBB
  G. W. 48,49,
52
  Geo. W. 4,10,
26,37,38,44(2),
47,48(2),52
  George 51
  George W. 1,4,
10,15,16,18,23,
44,45,51
  Gorge W. 15
  Hester 48
  Jane 43

COBB (Cont.)
  Shade 49
  Shadrick 48
COFFIELD
  Alfred 47
  Benjn. 48
  Deliah 47
  Delilah 48
  Elizabeth 45,
51
  Harriet 43
  Jacob 43
  John 45
  Luke 51
COGGAN
  Winiford 47
  Wm. G. 47
COLLINS
  Elizabeth 52
  William 52
COMPTON
  J. W. 46-48,
50(3),51
  Jas W. 51
COOPER
  Adaline 48,52
  Asa 49,52
  Edward 52
  Eliza 43
  Elizabeth 49
  H. C. 37,47,
48,52,53
  Henry C. 32,
36,37,49
  Henry D. 46
  Henry G. 50
  King 48,52
  Letty 53
  Lizzie 52
  Rebecca 48
CORBET
  Frank 50
CORBIT
  Frank 46
COSTIN
  Cary 52
COTTON
  Janice 45
  Lewis 45
  Pattie C. 45
COX
  R. E. L. 3,48
  Re E. L. 16
  Richard E. L.
3,16,26,46
  Richd. E. L. 46
CRAIG
  A. M. 4,10,11,
19(2),22,44-46,
50(3)
  James 49
  Mary Ann 50
  Rosetta 49
CREASY
  Jack 50
  Lucy 50
CROOKS
  R. N. 12,21,
27,33
  CULIPHER
  Fannie 51
  Simon 51
CULLIPHER
  James 50
  Rebecca 50

-D-

DANIEL

DANIEL (Cont.)
  Eli 46
  Fannie 46
DAVIS
  Aaron 51
  Nancy 51
  Rebecca 45
DEBREAUX
  Moses 46
DEMPSEY
  Bill 44
  Dossey 50
  Elizabeth 47
  Jackson 51
DEMPSY
  Anna 50
  James 50
  Jessee 48
  Mary 50
  Serapan 51
  Whitmelle 47
DICKSON
  David 43
  Eldern 43
DISON
  Ben 46
DONALDSON
  Margaret 52
  Penina 50
  Peninah 49
  Peniny 44
  William 44,49,50
DOSSEY
  Abram 45
  Rebecca 45
DOUGLAS
  Bettie 49
  George 49
DOWNING
  G. W. 15,43,48(3)
  Geo. 30
  Geo. W. 20,21,30,39,43-47
  George 30
  George W. 15,39
DRAKE
  Wm. 44
DUNDALOW
  John 43
DUNDERLOW
  Eliza E. 43
  John 43
DUNNING
  Antenett 48
  Emma 43
  Harriet 49
  Lazarus 49
  Ned 48
  Wiley 43

-E-

EASON
  Alfred 45
  George 51
  Mary 51
EBUN
  Luther 49
EICHE
  James 47
ELLYSON
  Lewis 49
EPPS
  Henry 46
  Penelopy 46
ETHERIDGE
  Debora 45
EVANS
  Celia 52
  Freeman 52
  James 43,47
  Mary 43,45-47
  Starky R. 46
EVINS
  Edwin 45
EVRITT
  Richard 47

-F-

FAGANS
  Amanda 49,50
  Henry 49,50
FANNING
  Silva 47
FLOOD
  Mary 45
FLOYD
  Mary 43
  Samuel 43
FOLK
  Judy 43
FREEMAN
  Bryant 48
  George 43
  John 52
  Mary 52
  Nelly 48
  Samuel 53
  Simon 47
  Violet 43
  Winney 53

-G-

GARDNER
  Cherity 44
GARRETT
  Anichy 50
GILLAM
  Arter 46
  Ceasor 46
  E. R. 50
  Guye 45,51
  Mat 52
  Matilda 46
  Moses 50
  Rachel 45,51
  Wilie J. 50
GORDEN
  Edward 46
  Nancy 46
GRAY
  Cherry 48
  Plato 48
GREEN
  G. N. 11,45,47,48,49(2),50,52
  Geo. N. 11,24
  George 52
  George N. 11
  Jenny 52
  Noah E. 47
  Susan 47
GREGORY
  David 44
  Sarah 44
GRIFFIN
  Clarisy 46
  Jim 43
  John B. 47
  Mary 43
  Sarah E. 47

-H-

HALE
  Joseph 43
HALL
  John H. 45
  Margaret Y. 45
HARDIE
  Winnie 52
HARDY
  Alfred 52
  Carrie 46
  Thos. B. 46
HARGRAVE
  Nancy 47
HARRELL
  Catherine 52
  David 15,30,31,45(3),49,50,51(2),53
  James 46
  Lisha 46
  Lucy E. 51
  Mary 43,51

HARRELL (Cont.)
  Noah 43,51
  Patience 48
  Rosetta 50
  Thomas 43
HARRIS
  George 46
HARRISSON
  Penelope 46
HAYS
  Fanny 45
HECKSTALL
  Chaney 44
  Hannah 44
  Harry 44
  Lucky 43
HENDRIX
  Anthony 44
  Mariah 44
HENRY
  Charles 49
HINES
  ——— 45
HOBBS
  Joseph 46
  Mary 46
HODGE
  Minnie 50
HOGGARD
  Bill 44
  Calvin 52
  David 46
  Jane 44
  Jennet 52
  Ludia 49,50
  Minor 49,50
  Nancy 45
  Rebecca 46
  Thomas 21
  Thos. 21,22,31
HOLDER
  Reddick 46
HOLLAMAN
  Joseph 18
HOLLAND
  Harriet 45
  Henry 45
HOLLEY
  David 49
  Patsy 49
HOLLOMON
  David 52
  Emily M. 50
  Isom 43
  Jane 52
  Joseph 43
  Priscilla 52
  Whitmill 50
  William 52
HUGER
  John 50
HUGHES
  James 51,52
  S. T. 14,24,35-37,48
  Sarah 51,52
HUGHS
  S. T. 14
HULL
  Austin 52
HUNT
  Lawson 49
  Rachel 49
HUSON
  Elizabeth 52
  John 52
HYMAN
  Jordan 50
  Martha J. 51
  William 51

-I-

None

-J-

JAMES
  Anthony 52
  Nancy 52
JENKINS

JENKINS (Cont.)
  A. 51
  Dick 51
  George 46,49
  James O. 43
  Jarsey 43
  Joseph 47
  Mary 46,49
  Nat 46
  Patsy 47
  Rhoda 47
  Sally 43
JERNIGAN
  Alfred 47
  Celia 49
  Drucilla 43
  Elizabeth 44
  George 49,50
  Sally 47
  William 43,44,46
JOHNSON
  A. 46
  Ben 45
  Daniel 51
  David 46
  Eliza 46
  Elizabeth 47
  Enoch 49
  Hanibel 47
  Jack 46,47
  Plesant 51
  Rachel 45,46
  Rebecca 47
  Winny 49
JONES
  Barbry 49
  Britton 45,50
  Celia 49
  Dossey 49
  George 49
  Isabella 45,50
  Miles 51
  Minney 47
  Silvy 49
  Willis 49
JORDAN
  Charles 43

-K-

KEETER
  John 47
  Sallie 47
KENEDY
  Mary 50
KENIDY
  Baldy 50
KING
  Benjn. F. 48

-L-

LANE
  George W. 46
  Katie 46
LANGDALE
  Hannah 53
LANGLEY
  Ann 47
  James 47
LANSTON
  Martin 44
LAUGHFORD
  James 45
LAW
  Pennie 49
  Peter 49
LAWRENCE
  Abner 51
  Levi 53
  Martha A. 51
  Robert 53
  Sallie 53
  Sallie Ann 53
LEARY
  Mary Ann 44
  Miles 44
LEE (See also LEW)
  Bob 43,50
  Bryant 1,2(2),

LEE (Cont.)
  Bryant (Cont.)
  3,7,8(2),9,11,12,13(2),16,19-21,23(2),25(2),29(2),30,31(2),32,33,34(2),37,38,39,43(3),44(4),45(4),46,47(3),48(3),50,51(5),52,53
  Byant 8
  David 44
  Delia 45
  James 52
  Jessee 43
  Nancy 44
  Olive 52
  Patsy 43,50
  Sarah 43
LEGGETT
  Nebuchadnezer 45
  Penicy 45
LENIER
  Frances 47
LEUS
  Jos. 51
LEVEN
  Henry 45
LEW (See also LEE)
  Bryant 11
LEWIS
  Watson 43,47,50(2),52(2)
LITTLETON
  Jerry 50
  Tobitha 50
LUKE
  J. M. C. 49

-M-

MABIN
  Abram 21,24,28(2),30,35,37
MC DANIEL
  James 51
  Orpy 51
MC GLAUHON
  George 44
  Susan 44
MARDRE
  Andy 48
MARRISS (See also MORRISS)
  Mary 50
MASON
  Abby 51
  Henry 51
  Milly 47
  Robert 50
  Speaker 47
MATTHEWS
  Jacob O. 52
  Sallie 52
MAVIN
  Abram 21
MEBANE (See also MABIN, MAVIN, MEBIN)
  A. W. 9
  Abram 10(2),11,12,20,41,43(2),44,47,51(2),52
  Allin 48
  Amelia 48
  Andy 45
  Cherry 43
  Chovey 52
  Marina 49
  Nathan 49
  Sabra 45
  Toney 43,52
  Venus 49
MEBIN
  Abram 28
MELTON
  Weston 43
MILES
  Benjn. 46
  Charlotte 46

MILLER
  David 46
  Dempsey 45
  Hanabell 52
  John 49
  Mary 43
  Penelope 49
  Sarah 46
  Solomon 43
  Tempy 47
MINTON
  Byrum 47
  Sarah 47
MITCHELL
  Ann Mariah 44
  Ben 51,52
  Bryant 44
  Cherry 52
  Daniel 47
  Dossey 51
  Elisha 48
  G. M. 47
  Hannah 51
  J. G. 47
  John 3,4(2),7,
8,10,12-14,19,21,
22,24,27,28(2),
29,32,33,41,43,
44(2),46,50
  John G. 7,9-11,
18,25,34,36-38,
43(2),45,47(4),48,
52(2)
    King 46
    Mary 48
    Petina 51
    Rebecca 46
    Sarah 46
    Sip 51
    Winnie 51
MIZELL
  Cyntha 50
  Delily 49
  Eady 49
  James 45,50
  Josiah 47
  M. L. 6
  Mary 49,51
  Moses 47
  Moses L. 4,
6(2),10,12,19,
25(2),29,39,41,
43(2),46(3),51
    Mosses L. 6
  Nancy 47
  Syntha 45
  Thos. 49
MOORE
  Anney 51
  Cherry 52
  George 49
  Harriet 43
  Jerry 43
  Maken 51
  Moses 49
  Sallie 49
  Sarah 49
MORING
  Carry 52
  Jordan 50
  Zed 52
MORRIS
  Harry 48
MORRISS (See also
MARRISS)
  Allen 47
  Ben 50
  Caron 48
  Harry 50
  James L. 46,48
  Jane 45
  John 50
  Kerron 46
  Mary 50
  Ned 47
  Sally 47
MOUNTAIN
  Beter 24
  P. 48
  Peter 8,13(2),
17-19,20(2),22,

MOUNTAIN (Cont.)
  Peter (Cont.)
23,24,26(2),27(2),
28,30,31,34,36(2),
42,43(2),44(2),
45(3),46,47
MOUNTAN
  Peter 26

-N-

NEWBERN
  John 51
NEWSOM
  Joseph 48
NICHOLLS
  Bob 50
  Gilbert 52
  Hester 50
  Martha 45
  Moses 49
  Penelope 49
  Solomon 45
  Thomas B. 45
NORFLEET
  Anthony 43
  Harriet 43

-O-

OUTLAW
  Alexander 52
  Alfred 45(2)
  Ben 45,47,49
  Bettie 53
  Bob 49
  Drew 49
  George 46
  Henry 45,53
  Isaac 53
  James 45
  Kiddy 52
  Leah 50
  Lucy 45(2)
  Magaet 45
  Marina 44(2)
  Polly 49
  Rachel 45,49
  Simon 50
  Turner 44(2)
  Wilson 44

-P-

PARKER
  Elizabeth 46,49
  Emeline 45
  Emily 51
  Frusy 44
  Henry 44
  John 45,51
  Laml 49
  Samuel 46
PEARCE (See also
PIEARCE,PIERCE)
  Edd. 52
  Edward 49,50
  Edwd. 50
  Hardy 48
  Hester 48
  Mary 47
  William 47,48
PEELE
  Essex 45
  Ned 45,51
  Rose 45,51
  Violet 45
PELT
  Cooper 45
  Mariah 45
PERRY
  Andrew 49
  Daniel 49
  Dossey 47
  Esther 49
  George W. 46
  Lavena 48
  Lavenia 50
  Levina 44
  Martha A. 46
  Martin 44,48,50

PERRY (Cont.)
  Moring 49
  Nancy 49
  Rachel 47
  Rose 49
  Violet 49
  Wm. 44
PERVIS
  George 51
PETERSON
  Emanuel 45
  Matilda 45
PHELPS
  Ann Rebecca 45
  Asa 49
  Elizabeth 49
  Jackson 44
  John 49
  Mary 52
  Micajah 45
  Milly 44
  Susan 49
  William 52
PIEARCE
  Edward 35
PIERCE (See also
PEARCE,PIEARCE)
  Edward 35,
39(2),40(3)
PITMAN
  Z. 47
POWELL
  Aaron 43
  Adaline 47
  Croford 44
  Dempsy 48
  James M. 17
  Jim 45
  Martha 44,45
  Mary 48,52
  Phebe 43
  Rhoda 48
  Richard 48,52
  Wm. 47
PRICE
  John 47
  Sally 47
PRITCHARD
  Outlaw 45
PRUDEN
  Edward 44
PUGH
  Abram 51
  Adaline 47
  Aggy 46
  Alfred 47
  Alsey 50
  Arch 46
  Celia 46
  Harriet T. 49
  Hosea 50
  Jack 48
  Knowledge 51
  Mariney 52
  Peggy 51
  Phillis 44
  Rachel 46
  Rebecca 44
  Robbin 50
  Samuel 44,48
  Silas 52
  Solomon 46
  Will 46
  Wm. A. 49
PUTNEY
  Mary Ann 50

-Q-

None

-R-

RASCOE
  Annis 49
  Antony 51
  Arthur 51
  Cody 51
  Daniel 51
  Fairiba 48
  Granvil 47

RASCOE (Cont.)
  Granville 47
  Hetty 43,
47(3)
  Jack 43
  Norras 51
  Notice 51
  Susan 48
  William 52
RAWLS
  Mary 49
  Moore 49
RAY
  Emanuel 15
RAYE
  Hester 49
  Jacob 53
  Penny 53
RAYFORD
  Emma 44
  Johnson 44
RAYNER
  Cyntha 45
  James T. 49
  Jas. T. 48,49
  Sintha 47
RAYNOLDS
  Emanuel 45(2)
READY
  Dempsy 52
RENALDS
  Emanuel 48
RENOLDS
  Emanuel 53
REYNOLD
  Emanuel 20,23
REYNOLDS
  Emanuel 23,26,
38
  Emanul 26
  Imanuel 30
  Immanuel 32(2)
  Manuel 30
RHODES
  Alfred 44
  Elizabeth 51
  M. C. 22,28,
29,34
  Phillis 49
  Thomas 49
  Tom 47
  Wm. G. 51
RICE
  Hannah 44
  Harriet 44
  John 43
  Sarah M. 43
ROBBINS
  Bob 45,46
  Edward 50
  Hannah 45,46
  Violet 50
ROBERTSON
  Martha 51
  William 51
ROBINSON
  Fanny 43
  George 46
  Jo 43
ROSS
  Isaac 47
  Perneny 47
RUFFIN
  Adam 44
  Bettie 48
  Bynum 44
  Daniel 51
  Davy 43
  Easter 44,46
  Ephraim 44,46
  Harriss 50
  Hasty 43
  Lucky 50
  Marina 50
  Mary 44
  Milly 52
  Patint 44
  Patsy 51
  Patterson 44
  Sabry 48
  Silvia 44

RUFFIN (Cont.)
  Solomon 48
  Winnie 46
RYON
  Dave 43
  Ganvill 43
  Mary A. 43

-S-

SESSOMS
  J. W. 2,4,5,
11,16,26,27,47,
49(2),50,52
  John 43
  John W. 1,4,5,
11,14,16(3),17(2),
23(2),26,27,37,38,
44(2),45-47,50,51
SESSONS
  Jno. W. 48
SHARROCK
  Aaron 46
  Isam 45
SHAW
  Frances 45
  James 45
  John 45
  Neonia 45
SHEPPERD
  J. 2
  John L. 2
SHERROD
  Martha 43
  Washington 43
SIKES (See also
SYKES)
  Abner 53
SINGLETON
  Rebecca 47
  Roscoe 47
SKILES
  Jonathan 50
SKIRVIN
  Thos. W. 50,51
SMALL
  Donaldson 43
  Penelope 43
SMALLWOOD
  Ben 50
  Charles 47
  Eady 51
  Frank 51
  Harriet 47
  James 50
  Liszina 48
  Lizzina 52
  Martilla 51
  Milly 51
  Moses 51
  Priscy 50
  R. W. 8
  Renda 50
  Robert W. 8
  Robt. W. 5,6
SMITH
  Elijah 50
  Eliza 50
  Granville 50
  J. W. 7,23,24,
35,47(2),50-53
  James 44
  James H. 45
  James W. 47,49
  Jo 43
  John 50
  Nancy 44,50(2)
  Sally 43
SMITHWICK
  Hasty 50
  Martha A. 49,51
  Samuel 49,51
SPELLER
  Amanda 43,46
  Duran 43
  Eady 47
  Gain 43
  George 47
  Oscar 47
  Patience 47
  Wright 51

SPIVEY
    Caroline 45
    Celia W. 52
    Cinthy 45
    George 45
    Mariah 50
    Sarah 52
    Solomon 52
    Thompson 50
SPRUELL
    David 53
    Nicie 53
STEPENSON
    Daniel 43
STEPHENSON
    Cherry 43(2)
    Daniel 43
SUTTON
    Margaret 53
    Nelly 50
SWAIN
    Solomon 52
    William 48
SYKES (See also SIKES)
    Eliza 53

-T-

TASWELL
    Edward 49
    Eliza 49
TAYLOE
    Blount 44
    Chance 52
    Eliza 48
    Jane 52
    Jonathan S. 49
    Lawrance 48
    Mary 44
    Nancy 48
    Peggy 44
    Prudence 49
    Richard R. 44
TEAMER
    Emeline 45
    Jack 45
TEENCE
    Jacob 43
    Margarett 43
THOMAS
    Bob 44
    Elizabeth 43
    Everett 43
THOMPSON
    Amos 47
    Cato 52
    Diner 46
    Hampton 46
    James 52
    Lewis 47
    Margaret A. 47
    Rachel 52
    Titus 51
    Winnie 47
TODD
    Basha 49
    Elisha 49
    Hardy 48
    John 44
    Levina 44
    Sally 48
TOMS
    Charles 49
TORVELL
    Hannah 47
TRAVATHAN
    John E. 50
    Pleasant 50
TREADWELL
    Sarah 46
TYLER
    Celia 51
    George 47
    Perry C. 51
    Ralph 50
    Sallie 47

-U-

URQUHART

URQUHART (Cont.)
    Annie 46
    Celia 49
    Luke 49
    Mary R. 47
    Richard A. 47

-V-

VALENTINE
    Betty 45
    Isaac 45
VEALE
    Henry 50

-W-

WADEN
    Jonathan 49
WALKER
    Jordan 49
    Martha A. 49
    Oscar 43
WALTON
    Penelope 48
    Wm. 49,50(3), 51(3),52(2)
WARD
    Clem 49
    Clora 52
    Dembry 46,51
    Fannie 52
    Frank 52
    Isaac 43,46
    J. H. 6
    James H. 3,4, 6(3)
    Jas. H. 6
    Mariah 48
    Maura 52
    Rachel 46
    Sallie 51
    Sarah E. 46
    Starky 52
WATFORD
    Droy 45
WATSON
    Dick 44,47,53
    Harry 43
    Jane 43
    John 44
    Mariah 45
    Marrah 52
    Mary Jane 48
    Murow 43
    Rachel 46
    Rose 44
    Tempy 47
WEBB
    Logan 47(2)
    Lucinda 47
    Lucindy 47
    Mary 50
WEST
    Ellen 50
    Mead 50
    Patient 47
WESTON
    Ann 44
    George 44
WHEELER
    Lucinda B. 50
    Saml. J. 50
WHITAKER
    51
WHITE
    Abner 49
    Caroline 49
    David 47
    Emily 50
    Hannah 45
    Harriet 43,46, 50
    Harrison 51
    Harvey J. 43
    Hasty 43
    Henry 48
    Jacob 50
    James 52
    Josiah 46
    Julia 44

WHITE (Cont.)
    Kader 46
    Katy 49
    Lewis 45,47,48
    Louisa 48
    Louiza 50
    Ludy 46
    Luke 44
    Marina 47
    Martha 46,48, 51
    Martha A. 43
    Medea 48,51
    Nelson 49
    Penelope 44
    Sallie 43,52
    Sophia 48
    Starky 50
    Tempy 51
    Thos. 49
    Tom 43
    Vilett 47
    William 46,49
    Wright 49
WHITUS
    Caty 45
    Peter 45
WIGGINS
    Violet 51
WILDER
    Mary 52
    Mitchell 52
WILIBER
    Lavina 51
WILKINS
    Abby 49
WILLFORD
    Absaley 45
    Elizabeth 47
    John 45
    Robert 47
WILLIAMS
    Aggy 52
    Alfred 53
    Ann 52
    Annis 49
    B. B. 4,5,7-10, 20,24,26,28,36,38, 41,43(3),44,46(3), 48-50,52(2)
    Benj. B. 9
    Charles 52
    Cornelius 52
    Drew 43
    Elizabeth 52
    Esther 49
    Freeman 45,46
    Harriet 51
    Joanna 53
    John 51
    Katy 43
    Lewis 52
    Mary 47
    Mima 46
    Ned 52
    Penelope 46
    Penny 44
    Phillis 52
    Robert 49
    Serena 48
    Solomon 47
    Thos. 47
    Turner 50
WILSON
    Alfred 45
    Lucky 50
    Thad. 3,5,26, 29
    Thaddeus 1, 49(2),50(3),51(2), 52(2)
    Thadeous 1,3, 5,7(2),24,25(2), 41(2)
    Thadeus 2(2), 5(2),7,44(2), 45(2),46
WINSON
    Harreald 49
WOOD
    Harriet 49

WOOD (Cont.)
    Mary 45
    Richard 45
WOOLERD
    Major 45
WOOTEN
    Ed. 51
    Edd. 51
    Edwd. 47(2),51
WOOTTEN
    Edward 1,2,3(2), 15,19,22(2),33,37, 39,43
    Edwd. 45(2),49(2)
    Mary E. 49
    Shadrick 49
WORTHINGTON
    Elizabeth 50
    Robt. H. 50
WYNNS
    Deliala 52
    Nancy 44
    Ned 44,51
    Penny 52

-X-

None

-Y-

None

-Z-

None

INCOMPLETE NAMES

    Benjamin 40
    Bryant 19
    Edward 39
    Edwootten 33
    Nathan 46
    Solomon 49

www.ingramcontent.com/pod-product-compliance
Lightning Source LLC
Chambersburg PA
CBHW040223040426
42333CB00051B/3427